CW00847563

DUDE
~*OUR COVER HORSE*~

Submitted By MISSY

◆ ◆ ◆

D

D ude was a skinny, sad looking palomino sitting in pen 10 of November 2015 when Cranbury shared him on their Facebook page. There were 3 horses in there that I liked, my cousin Tammy said I should get the skinny one he has the best video. So I paid the 500$ fee and brought him home to Washington Pa. There was no reason for him being skinny other than neglect.

We decided on the name Dude because he's just so chill. After we quarantined him for 3 months, I brought him to the Meadows Racetrack and Casino to get shoes on him, and he seemed un-phased by the whole Racetrack life.

I been the outrider there for the last 20yrs, a lot of my horses come from sales or pens. I decided to start training him to outride.

Fast forward 3yrs later Dude is on his way to being one of the top outriding horses in harness racing. He's caught a couple loose horses, let's the kids carrying flags off him during the big races. Even rode at the Little Brown Jug with crowds over 50,000 and never bats a eye.

He's still as sweet as can be and loves attention from all his fans. He's know in harness racing as the Barbie Dream Horse!

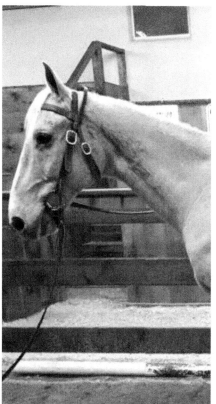 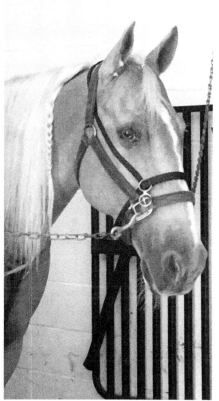

❖ ❖ ❖

ATHENA

Submitted by JEN

I rescued Athena in May of this year from the Sunnyside, Wa. Feedlot.

There are a group of ladies that go to the feedlot take pictures of the horses, throw a saddle on them to see if they've been ridden, then they post the pictures and videos on their fb page to try and save them.

I saw this sweet girl on their page and knew I had to go get her. She's an ottb who's tattoo had been ground off. She was skinny, beat up, and defeated. She's the sweetest girl...no clue how she could have ended up there with 2 days to live.

After getting her health back...this was my 4th time on her with just a liberty loop. I got a dna kit from the jockey club and we found her! So fun. She is 14 years old and her Jockey Club name is Free Smiles. She is my third rescue horse and such a gentle spirit.

Thanks for shining a light on the rescues!

◆ ◆ ◆

BARNEY

Submitted by Scott

I was a cowboy at a feed lot in Texas when I met my wife Melissa. We both loved the country life and loved horses. We bought a decent size ranch and had several good ranch horses. We were NOT looking to add any more. Until Barney.

As luck would have it, I was driving some cattle to the pen from a shipment that had just come in. I look down and see this foal standing among the cattle. I called my boss and told him, and was told to keep driving him with them, he was going with the lot to the "house",(what some of us call the slaughter facility.

No way was I doing that, I told my boss I would cut him out and buy him, and of course the boss didn't care as long as it didn't interfere with work. So I got him into a pen alone and called Melissa, who was working the scale house and told her about the foal. She rushed down to the pen and immediately went to work herding him into a smaller pen so we could catch him and give him the once over.

He was a straggly little fella who was the prettiest red roan I had ever seen! Well, after work we ran him into a trailer and took him home. We had a long weekend off of work so we got the vet out and had him looked over, and he was a bit under-weight but in good shape otherwise. The vet said he was only a few moths old, and still needed a bottle! HA! We had our work cut out for us, BUT we had a mare who had just lost her foal, and was still full of milk, but would she take him? After a very brief introduction, she nickered to him and he went right over and started drinking! I could not believe it! He would make it!

That was 5 years ago, and he is a gorgeous red roan geld-ing! Melissa and I both ride him, and work cattle with him. He has never been sick a day since we rescued him, and is built like a tank!

We finally found out how he ended up with the cattle though. He had been running with the ranchers herd, and was separated from his mom during the round up. AND he was a mustang! So the rancher looked at it as he was getting rid of a nuisance! Well, he is the BEST nuisance we have ever had!

BELLA

Submitted By LYDIA

Two years ago, I was living on a donkey sanctuary when we got a call on about a mule who was aggressive. The old couple who owned her need to get rid of Bella, so we go take a look and finally took her home a couple of weeks later. She wasn't really handled, so it was hard to get her on the trailer and a bomb when she got out! She was soaked and wet, a lot of muck get out of her nostril and when she coughed a lot came out by the mouth too!

When she calmed down it was time to introduce her in the group, but unfortunately she got scared so much by the donkey (she had never seen any before, only horses) I had the idea to put her with my filly .They fell in love right away! Bella is so protective ,she took Nelly on as her charge and is her bodyguard. Nelly liked her company right away too. She had lived all her life on a herd so she was happy to share her space with her.

In February, I began a job on a ranch and learned western riding because I did ride when I was young, but only a year and it was at an English dressage school.

In March, I moved my girls to the ranch to continue training Bella and with help on the ground I broke Bella myself with my month experience of riding. Today I laugh at myself to see how big the dream I had but I got it ..... Almost ..... Bella needed a britchen or a crouper at least to keep the saddle at the proper place and no one had experience with mules. Often we went for a ride and Bella just came to a dead stop. How many times I flew over her head and take her back with the saddle on her neck , easy 6-7 times and surely more.

We finally put a crouper on,but it was to much pressure on her little tail. I had the Idea to trick a harness britchen on the saddle and it worked well, but horse saddle didn't fit her either. Her back is so

straight that the curve on the tree hurt her poor back . It was hard to find a saddle maker who wanted to help me, but finally I got a custom made saddle and the result made a whole new mule!

We began to compete this summer in pleasure, horse-manship and gymkhana. We brought back 7 ribbons in 4 competitions ! She hates bits as well, so now she rides in hackamore and it seems to me that she likes it more than a bit!

BLUESKYES THE LIMIT

Submitted By RACHEL

I t was July of 2018, and I was just browsing on Facebook when a picture of a black mare showed up on my news feed. She was a local rescue that was advertising her. A friend of mine on Facebook had already "loved" the picture of her. Something about her picture just caught my eye. I had to know more about her. So I commented asking for more info. And what I found out just about broke my heart. BluSkye was estimated to be between 5-8 years old.

She was rescued from a case of neglect, hoarding, and plain old animal abuse. She was part of a herd of about 100 or so horses that were running amuck on a woman's farm. The fences were non existent, there was no access for water, no evidence of hay or grain. Among these horses were stallions that were breeding all of the mares. When BluSkye came in she had a 2 year old colt attached to her, both were in horrible shape. All of them were in horrible shape. I hadn't owned a horse in 5 years. Hadn't even thought about owning a horse until I saw this mares photo. The colt was young so he found a home quickly. But poor BluSkye was being overlooked over and over again.

I went and visited her, not expecting much. But what I found was love at first sight. She didn't know anything, she barely knew how to walk on a lead, she didn't know what a brush was, she knew humans meant food. But that was it. I had fallen in love with a basically feral horse. I went and visited with her 2 more times. And then I made my decision.

August 3rd, the day before my birthday, I signed the papers and arranged for a horse trailer. I was terrified. I didn't know how I was going to get this horse to load. When she was just starting to get used to me grooming her. I got there about an hour before the trailer was suppose to arrive. I started grooming her like I normally do and decided to just walk her around. The trailer came and it was the moment of truth. The owner of the farm asked if I wanted him to load

BluSkye. I said no I wanted to try. He didn't have much faith in my ability but he didn't argue. We start walking towards the trailer... and up she went. She followed me right into that trailer without a second

thought. It was amazing. And nobody could believe that she went so quietly. We had about a 30 minute drive to her new home. And all the while I'm thinking to myself "I hope she doesn't freak out too much when I take her off. A new place, new smells, she's going to be scared". When we got to the barn I opened the trailer to get her off, and to my amazement she walked as calm as could be off the trailer, down the aisle way and right into the stall. The lady who owns the farm who allows me to board there said something that I think to this day is still true. She said "once you earn the trust of a horse with an uneasy past, you'll never have to worry." In just those 3 visits that I had with BluSkye before loading her I had already gained her trust.

Fast forward 3 months after bringing her home... BluSkye, which is now BluSkyesTheLimit, allows full body grooming, stands for bathes, beginning to stand to have her feet picked up, lunges on a lunge line with a surcingle and draw reins, takes the bit like she's done it her whole life, allows polo wraps/boots on her legs, and has shown a talent for jumping! My plan for the beautiful girl is dressage and hunter jumpers. If I'm brave enough. Perhaps cross country. Because... the skies the limit for BluSkye. And I can't imagine my life without her.

DECLAN

Submitted By KELLY

I think we often think of a "rescue horse" as that downtrodden, skinny, wounded, or sickly horse standing lifelessly in a pen. I think we often forget that sleek, round, bright eyed horse standing looking directly into the camera is not always the first to get snapped up. He is not the first to get all of the attention. He is not the first to be saved from shipping to Canada or Mexico. Afterall, "someone else will probably grab that one" right? What about "oh there must be something wrong with that one.... He looks too good to be standing in the kill pen". "What's the catch?" All things horsemen/women have said, including myself.

Every day, people have their little Monday morning routines. Some work out, some hustle to make it to work and school on time, some sip coffee while scrolling the modern day newspaper; social media. For horse people, that often includes scrolling through the countless sale, auction and rescue ads for horses. Whether you are in the market for a horse or not, I think we all do it.

My Monday was just like this in August of 2018. I looked forward to seeing the Monday pictures of the horses that would be presented for sale on Wednesday evening at the Cranbury auction in New Jersey.

I didn't really need another horse...well.... We COULD use a lesson horse.... Did we really "need" one????? Well, maybe if the right one came along.

The lies we tell ourselves. Per the usual, there were all types, skinny ones, fat ones, pretty ones... not so pretty ones, tall ones, short ones. I always pick a few that I like and make sure to follow up Tuesday just to see their videos out of curiosity. One particularly

caught my eye. Number 026. He was listed as a 15.3h, QHX 13yr old gelding and that he was a "well broke gelding that rode english and

western and jumped a small course, knows both leads and frames up. "Yeah right" as I thought about all the horrible things he probably does and the reason why he has landed in this predicament. I closed my laptop and went about my day.

For someone who "doesn't need another horse", especially a widow maker like I was sure he was, I was johnny on the spot to check out his video Tuesday. He was ridden in a western saddle and was shown at the walk, trot and canter both directions. He moved well. He was obedient, had a soft, eager and expressive expression, had great cadence to his gaits and worked effortlessly through his transitions all with a soft and relaxed head and neck. I think I watched it at least a dozen times. I sent it to every horse friend and professional I could think of. They all had some sentiment of "oh my gosh, he is adorable...... what's the catch". Throughout the day, I had variances of feelings. "Should I do it", "What if he is terrible", "could he be drugged" and "what do I do". I have never purchased a horse sight unseen off of an auction. I was not sure I was in a position to take such a financial risk..... But he WAS already fat and shiny... there would not be that cost...

The lies we tell ourselves.

One thing that puzzled me about this horse is he had no chatter on his picture nor his video. Pretty and sleek horses always garnish many "likes" and comments. This guy had a few likes and no

comments. Through doing a little research ahead of time, I figured out that he had also been run through the New Holland sale the week before but obviously did not sell."hmmm maybe they want too much money for him". I secretly hoped that was the case. I mean, that is what would keep him safe right? I was being silly. Sleek and shiny horses don't end up in the kill pen..... right? Convinced that was probably the case and I would never be able to justify spending so much money on an auction horse, I shrugged the whole thing off. And yet I was back tuning in to watch the live stream of the sale that is done by a volunteer later that night. You know.. just out of curiosity.

I watched all shapes and sizes run through. A three legged lame mare was even led through. She was sad, so thin and so painful. She was sent to the #10 pen, the pen that is set to ship to Canada. I only hoped that she would be one of those rescues you hear about getting pulled from the kill pen. Even if it only meant to have a dignified ending surrounded by love. Then number 026 came up. By comparison, his brilliant chestnut coat made him look more like he was walking into the show ring rather than the kill sale. Little did he know, this could have been the most important show of his life. My heart was racing so hard you would think the Kentucky Derby was about to start. The price ran up. The price ran down. No comments came across the live stream. No one bid. No one did anything. Within a few moments, it was over. "No Sale! #10 pen 026". I could not believe what just happened and I began to REALLY doubt what I was

seeing in this horse. I felt like I was seeing something no one else was. After a few minutes of full blown panic and indecision, I decided to reach out to someone who I knew was there... you know.... Just out of curiosity. She ended up striking up a deal for me and by 10:30 that night I owned another horse.

He ended up going to quarantine about 45 days just to be safe. We gave him the name Declan and Declan handled his QT like a champ. He was friendly and polite which was a welcome reprieve considering I was pretty convinced he HAD to be drugged since sleek and shiny horses do not end up in the kill pen for no reason, right?. After dodging hurricane Florence and the roads were passable, he was able to make the trip home to Florida. After 20 hours on the trailer, I expected him to be a full blown dragon especially considering he had minimal turn out before heading down. Much to my suprise, he came off of the trailer, looked around at the construction going on at my farm and began grazing. We decided to give him a few days to chill and relax and then we would have our local, 19 year old bronc rider come out to hop on him.

D-day arrived. We saddled him in an english saddle and turned him loose in the round pen. We stood waiting for him to explode and fold in two like he thought he was in the NFR. but.... He didn't. He walked, trotted and cantered obediently without even as much as a head shake. I found myself with a half of a smarmy grin on my face as we led him to the arena. I wondered if I had just become one lucky gal but quickly squashed it with "just hold on there.... You just haven't

found the reason he was at the auction yet". My bronc rider got up on him and walked off. Within a few minutes he had walked, trotted and cantered and then done all three gaits on the buckle. Declan never changed his pace, never deviated off his riders course.Hmm. Maybe he is horrible or even dangerous to jump.
The rider began to skip him over small jumps and then allowed him to canter around the small course. Again, Declan never changed his pace other than to perk up a bit when he saw his distance, he never looked or spooked, or bucked or did anything wrong. Not one foot out of place.

It has been a little over 2 months that Declan has been here. He has done beginner kid lessons and has had more advanced riders ride and jump him. He has been trail riding, swimming and been ridden bareback. Declan has not put a single foot out of place. Like so many of them, someone DID love and care for him at some point, probably very recently even. Someone even cared enough about him to invest in his training. He is happy, friendly and silly. Absolutely Mr. Personality. I think we often get hung up on the rescues who look bad and may not realize the ones who are fat, shiny and well trained may be getting overlooked. So although Declan's story is not that of the traditional "rescue" story, his situation was no less dangerous. He was shoulder to shoulder with the three legged lame mare and no one originally came for either of them. The skinny and injured and the sleek and shiny would have taken that last ride together. Everyone says he is pretty lucky, but I think I got pretty lucky too.

◆ ◆ ◆

FROM THE HORSES MOUTH

Submitted By RAINBOWS EDGE RESCUE

H ello my name is TC. I heard a rumor Rainbows Edge had a place that I could talk to lots of humans and I want to share with you my HAPPILY EVER AFTER STORY. I know when you first start reading you may not see how this could be a happy story but please take the time and as I get further along I believe you will understand. I asked to talk to you because this time in my life has become very important to me. You see I went to see Dr Cooley this past week and they did many tests because my nose kept bleeding. The results came back and I have Cancer, I don't really know what that means but I was told all of you would. What I do understand is it is going to keep growing and the people here at Rainbows Edge know what to watch for so I do not have to live in pain. They said my meas-ured time left with all of you will not end in weeks but it will be in months. Now if you would please give me a few moments of your time I want to share my story with you. I was caught run-ning around by Animal Control, when they found me I had on a saddle and no pad, my back hurt so bad and it took them 2 days to catch me.

I was afraid, hungry,and my body hurt beyond belief. After they got me in the big metal box with wheels they brought me to a place and gave me food and took the saddle off. Then they contacted Fallen Oak Equine Rescue,I didn't know who these humans were but I got on the trailer and went with them all the time wondering what was going to happen to me next, do these humans take me to the place all horses hear about called the slaughter house? All the time in the trailer I prayed that was not the place I was going.

When I got off the trailer they brought me to grass ,they gave me clean water and a human named Korina touched me with the most gentle hand and told me I was safe and every thing was going to be alright. I stayed with her for a little while and them human Kim the lead human mare for Fallen Oak came and said they had a place called Rainbows Edge that wanted to meet me and help me find the strong confident horse they understood me to be.

At this time I was not worried that the humans around me were going to hurt me but I was nervous what they were going to want me

to do and are they able to communicate with me in a language I can understand which it horse. When I arrived I met a lot of people and there were lots of other horses. I met a special young human named Trainer Jessie .In the next week Human Kim found out so many things that have happened to me for the last 9 years and only for 2 months was it good. I had been pasted around by humans that did not understand horses and how to communicate or care for them , I was hungry many times and scared most of the time and yes at times experienced pain from them.

Human Kim did find out about my first 11 yrs of my life and that my name was TC. One day Trainer Jessie came to spend time with me and in stead of calling me by a name I didn't know she walked up to me and said TC I raised my head and looked at her closer. How does she know my name? Did I know you from a time when my life was wonderful? My time here at Rainbows Edge has been so wonderful, I feel loved and with the help of Trainer Jessie and all the volunteers here, I trust humans I have let go of my past because I know it is the past and I will never have to be afraid again. There is never a hard hand here it is always a gentle touch.I know I keep going on but this is my chance to talk to you so please bare with me a little longer.. I know now you must be asking how is this a Happily Ever After Story,I need to go back to the beginning.

I was bought for a 14 yr old girl when I was about 1 yr old We grew up together we trained together and we Barrel Raced together , We were always together we were best friends, I knew my job and she knew hers and we took care of each other I understood commitment ,trust and love and knew this was going to be my life that I loved and I would have my girl my whole life, Then one day I didn't see her and this happened day after day, I was missing her so much what happened where is my girl. Then one day my girls human Mom came and told me that my girl was gone to heaven and all I could think of was "Tell me where that is I will go and get her ".I cried day after day for my loss, I felt that I lost my whole world. She was only 24 and

passed from Cancer About 1 yr later My girls Mom said I was getting a knew home and you know every thing from there.

OK I will get to the Happily Ever After ....

A month ago for Christmas I got a Dad he adopted me he said he was going to make sure I never knew hunger or pain and he was going to be my knew best friend . I really trust him and he is so gentle with his touch, I can tell he cares about me. Even though he heard about my Cancer he is not returning me to Fallen Oak, he is going to stay my Dad.

I want to tell all you wonderful humans that support horse rescues Thank you, with out you this part of my life never would have happened,

I have one more thing and this is the Happily Ever After part. I know when its time for me to leave this ground you humans call earth they will call Dr. Cooley and he will help me so it will be quick and I will not have to stand in a pasture suffering in pain and until that time they are letting me stay in the pasture with the mares, they are my herd and I am a good leader. I will not feel hunger or thirst for water and I will stay groomed and loved until that time that I must say good bye, but listen this is the best part. When it is time please don't be sad because I know my Human Mom and Best friend is waiting for me in Heaven and I know she will be right there with her arms stretched to wrap them around my neck taking me from the loving arms of my Human Dad. So please don't cry for me that day but know I am again riding with my best friend that I have held in my heart all these years. I want to thank everyone that comments,shares ,volunteers and donates to rescues,you are all a part of the heart that beats and keeps the rescues and shelters alive..Thank you for giving me the time to share my story,When I get to heaven and meet the Angels I am going to tell them about all the Angles that live on earth there are so many of you.

GABRIEL

Submitted by CAITLIN

After having horses years ago I knew I wanted another but didn't know where to start. I was scrolling through Facebook one day when a shared post for Tarheel Feedlot came up. I was looking through the horses seeing in bold letters, LAST CHANCE TODAY! My eye caught a big chestnut gelding they called Bomber.

They advertised him as a 4 year old quarter horse, 15.3 and green as green could be. I watched his videos over and over where he had no clue what he was doing and didn't want to really move. I couldn't check soundness but I was in love. I watched the post all day waiting for someone to save him. Updates would come but not for him. I started messaging my husband about him and how we had to do something! (Mind you we are parents to four young kids, 7, 4, and 18 month old twins.

We have modest jobs and no farm.) He was hesitant bringing up valid points about not knowing what we were getting into, cost to board, feed, time, vet, farrier. I started calculating and doing everything to make it work on paper, he was still saying we can't do this. I said if I can work with him we can pull him to get him off the lot and I'll find a good home. It's 5pm and not a single offer on him and the post says 6pm deadline and I start to panic and plead my husband he knew I was serious. By 5:45pm the page updated to say, Bomber SAFE SAFE SAFE!

He was in NC and we are in VA so on went the job of getting him home and a place for him to go. Those 48 hours were so trying but we made it happen and on June 16th he was home! Underweight, scared and unsure he still had the kindest eye. I call vets and schedule him for an exam, she scores him a 4/10 with bad rain rot and a mysterious lump on the outside above the right knee. I'm told to "watch it" but otherwise he was healthy. A week after that was his first trim, he did not take well to it and after was dead lame on that same knee. We knew something was off but nothing was matching that type of injury.So he got lots of rest, love, lush grass, food and patience and he was blossoming. Afraid of all tack and pretty much anything and

unable to be tied I had a job on my hands. A few weeks later after he was still off and swelling remaining we got the vet out for x-rays, it only

took one to see that his accessory carpal joint was completely shattered. We were crushed, so sad for what he had endured at such a young age. But still he was just so loving and had our hearts.

I started doing my own research and found out he was born on a racing farm in Kentucky and wasn't a QH but a pure bred Thoroughbred! I called the barn he was born at and he was an orphan whose mother died during his birth. No one would say why but they then said he was thrown in a pasture for 3 years and then given away. That owner sold him 8 months later, and that owner sold him to the kill buyer. Turns out he is five and a son of Horse Greeley. He was never named, never registered, never raced. None of his prior owners would say what happened to him. So I left it at that. God had chosen me to pick him.

A few more weeks go by and one day I go out and the swelling is gone! I lunge him and he's completely sound. It just seemed like a miracle, the vets couldn't believe it! He now comes when called, follows me everywhere, and trusts whatever I do. It's like he knows he is finally HOME!

Our journey continues.. our accomplishment this week was getting a blanket on! Somehow it's like we have saved each other, I never knew I needed healing until I had him.

GUNNAR

Submitted by ALYSSA

This was my first rescue, Gunnar. I bought him from Camelot many years ago. I had been on a roller coaster with my other horse due to Navicular, and decided I would retire him (for the first time) and find another horse I could ride.

I had hunted around for the right horse, and got disheartened by a few people trying to hide things on sales horses I looked at. I didn't want to go to an auction, because I was afraid I would want to take them all home. Finally decided to give it a shot, but I drove up trailer less the night before the sale just to look, so I wouldn't be too tempted to buy. I walked into the sale barn, saw his spotted butt standing in one of the pens, and I knew he was mine.

Drove back the next day and bid on my first horse ever at an auction. The only one who bid against me was a kill buyer. I bid above him and took this horse home for $600. He thankfully went through quarantine uneventfully and came home.

Within the first week of him being home I took him to his first Hunter Pace. He was a saint and a half. He built my confidence and helped me branch out and try things I would have never with my other horse. But he wasn't meant to only touch my life. A trainer that came to the barn I kept him at had sadly just lost her two horses in a fire, along with the other 24 horses at that barn.

Eventually, both Gunnar and I joined the barn she trained out of, and I met Caitlyn. When I was struggling financially post college, she half leased him from me and he also became the barn's go to lesson horse. $600 but worth his weight in gold. This horse basically put back together a barn, a business, and a lot of people's broken hearts.

Unfortunately, he had recurrent uveitis and vision loss, and we lost him in a pasture accident a little over two years ago.

He will forever be the greatest thing to ever happen to me. After we lost him, my first horse thankfully had many more sound years left in him after surgery for his Navicular and we shared him for years as well. Now, a few years later, we had to make the decision to retire him

for the second time, and Cait and I together bought our rescue from the same auction house (now known as Cranbury.)

JESSE, A MORAB RESCUE FROM SEXTON'S

Submitted by RAELLE

His bail was paid by donations and I agreed to take him in. He came to us with a calcified pastern injury and strangles.

After he recovered from that he came home and bonded instantly with my mare Gypsy. They quickly became inseparable.

We set up a regime of chiropractic and specialty farrier work to ease his discomfort on the bad leg and for awhile, we saw huge improvements. Jesse opened up to us and was very social and sweet and talkative, eager to meet us and his herd mates, but was consistently seen watching over Gypsy and nuzzling her.

Suddenly he started losing weight and withdrawing from the herd and people. We did everything we could, but he was in pain as his joint began calcifying more, tipping his toe backwards.

His muscles wasted away on the side with the bad leg. Unfortunately we had to put him down, but at least he lived and loved well the last few months, including finding his one true love!

I'm glad we were able to give him a soft place to land after serving someone in the show ring for 14 years. We miss him. But I know he's finally running free and painlessly.

KHOSMO

Submitted By MEGAN

My name is Megan Knowles. I was Megan Burcham when I first got Khosmo, my first actual horse. I was 18 years old. I was going through a rough time with my family. I am adopted from Romania. I have seven siblings. Four of us adopted from Romania. The last three little blond haired girls were born from my mom and dad who adopted me. My mom and I had a bad relationship since I was 2 after getting adopted. Ever since my life has been sad and hard.

I couldn't be with the family because everyone knew mom hated me. I had to keep the peace by staying in my room. But because of Black Knight Stables, and their open heart,, had offered for me to come out to horse camps and come and ride and have fun since I was 8. I fell in love with horses.

But 2017 rolled in, this was my senior year. My dad forcing me to join the army,I wasn't sure of. I was scared of my dad after the things he had been doing to me. But I kept loving horses and trying for what reason I didn't know my life was falling all over the place, and my mom and I only getting along when we were alone. My siblings and I never had good connection since they didn't want to be hated by mom. A wonderful lady called me one day. I was 18 years old. Summer. 2017. I was introduced to Khosmo. He was a skinny and scared abused horse. He was a redish/brown arabian with a stripe down his face but near his right eye the stripe seemed to have a small chunk near his right eye on the stripe cut off a little. It was cute. His beautiful blond mane and tail with his Chestnut color. Made me love him more. His personality won me over as well. I loved underdogs. To be able to show the world a rusty machine and turn it to gold. But I was still learning to train horses. I had worked with horses since I was 8. So when I was able to bring Khosmo over with help from Black Knight Stables , who all communicated about keeping Khosmo there for me.

He was scared if you walked up to him fast. You couldn't throw a blanket on him, nor a saddle. It took slow and gentle work. My mom

had made me go to the barns on snow days when it was 0 below. I would bring Khosmo in and warm him up. Feed him and talk to him and keep warm under his blanket. Together we bonded and as

summer came I rode him. I couldn't turn him at first. He was almost trying to lay down. Stopping him was a nightmare! But slowly but surely he got there.

Even though our rides were five minutes long I learned about reining from watching a Reiner at our barns. It was amazing. He could teach a horse in seconds. I watched videos and him and to this day, Khosmo does immature reining. Khosmo earns his keep by his reining lessons. Everyone loves Khosmo. I have taught Khosmo a Indian whistle with my hands and he comes to it knowing theirs a treat somewhere. Giving others a hard to time to catch him, he know who his mom is. This horse made me a better person and see the light in a dark room. Even in zero below weather. Khosmo and I changed how people saw the both of us and we proceed the world wrong that the underdogs can go the distance. Because of Khosmo, I was able to keep my chin up and finish high school and to this day, when I'm not with my Army husband. I am living here visiting Khosmo as much as possible. With my Army husband taking care of me and our "son" Khosmo, I couldn't be happier. I love my horse and I owe him everything in the world. He has changed my life and I, his. With both poor pasts, we stood up together and showed the world what we were made of!

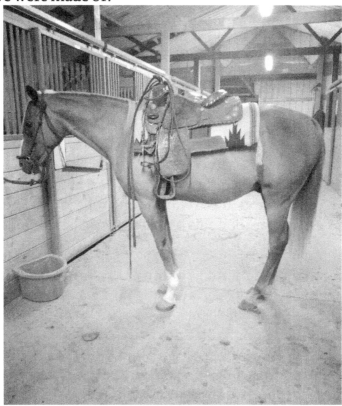

KNIGHTY KNIGHT

Submitted By SARALYN

He came off the nasty trailer from the guy that Larry got all his "flip" horses from. He was skinny and lame, but that wasn't a real shocker. I was looking more a the negative aspect of life because that's just how I was. I turned to the world of horses and this is our story.

This tall gelding WAS the skinniest that he'd ever picked up. He needed more than what the other horses needed. He was very bad off. Kelly went immediately to the feed store and started him on grain and Red Cell. Of course with our barn teamwork he started to gain weight. Then Larry turned him out to the pasture because visitors and guests were starting to "complain" about the skinny horse. So I just went out that huge pasture twice a day (rain, shine, heat and snow) to look for him and give him his grain and supplements. He eventually figured out his new routine and started meeting me at the gate! I called and updated Kelly with Knights' weight progress and she stated her concerns about maybe we can have the vet come out and take a look at him and see what else we can do. I told her that funds were excruciatingly low and wasn't quite sure how I can handle it. Through the tears and frustration, we decided to sleep on what we'd do and pray about it and hope that God guides us in the right direction to help this poor gelding.

A few days later, Larry came to me and said that if I stay and manage the barn and do good in my work I can HAVE the skinny Knight horse! He said he overheard me talking to Kelly the other night and said that he'd been thinking and said, "happy birthday!" So I quickly hooked the trailer up and went and got my new horse! I called Kelly and told her the good news! Knight had a real family!

We got him seen by a vet and even trimmed up by the farrier. He had to have front shoes because his feet weren't solid coffin bone, they had just deteriorated due to malnutrition. He didn't even have any

teeth to float, there was no growth because he didn't have the proper nutrients for the longest time. He estimated Knight to be about 18 years old. We continued with his grain plan and tweaked it a bit and after a couple months, Dr. Myers saw growth and better looking feet

(on the outside)! So he finally HAD feet to actually trim! Teeth to float and even little bit of back muscle to sit on! He was just the gentlest of souls! Big dark guy with the love and affection of a kitten! He let do almost anything to him! From paint to glitter to getting dressed up! He even became lesson-worthy from the trainer! He finally became trail-worthy after his shoes came off! That rice bran oil and Keretex Hoof Gel works wonders on hoofs! They are a staple in my barn now! Being an OTTB

I always wondered how he did on the track, and where he even came from. His tattoo was SO faded, only a couple small dots remained. His past didn't matter, though, as his future was just shining brighter than any star!

Tragedy struck when I got off late one night from work and went to go feed my horse he wasn't interested in eating his grain. Possible colic? Mouth sore? No. Stomach ulcers. Dr. Myers put him on some long-term medication which seemed to help the flare-ups. Then lameness again. Abscess. It was gross. He hurt for a while even after treatment. I felt terrible keeping him in his stall for long periods, day in and day out. It would heal, then another on the opposite foot. It was to the point of wrapping 3 different feet twice a day for almost weeks at a time. Dr. Myers said it was all the inside yuck finally coming out. He said he'd probably always have abscess very often. I guess I can handle wrapping and paying for his stomach meds, let's see what happens, maybe he'll grow out of his malnutrition. I didn't know what the hell I was doing. I just didn't want my baby boy to suffer. Kelly said that I was doing a great job and to keep at it for now. He may get better, right? Let's wait and see!

No. He didn't get better. He wouldn't eat, couldn't walk. What's a horse that can't even do what it would naturally do in the wild? What was I doing to him? In the dead of night, during the quiet still of the December moon, it hit me. I was selfish. I HAD to let him go. He was hurting.

After a long night of heartache and tears I called Dr. Myers when his clinic opened. He had me trailer him in for the sake of funds. He told me as far as my finances were concerned I would be better off

taking him to Valley Proteins in Warrenton, Virginia. I cried even harder as the thought of my precious baby going through that process. But Dr. Myers was right. I didn't own land, I couldn't afford to have him cremated. As the sad cold truth hit me, Miss Paige, his assistant, came to me with his tail in a neatly wrapped band. Dr. Myers said usually horses go thrashing about and making a lot of noises and ruckus when they go down. But not my sweet Knight. He said he went down as graceful as could be. Just laid down and went to sleep. Like he had been waiting for it all along. He was finally at peaceful rest. I said my final broken-hearted good-byes to my shiny Knight.

I continued on to Warrenton as per my instructions. The lady in the office told me they were expecting me and gave a box of tissues and told me to have a seat. There went the truck and the trailer back behind the building where I couldn't see. The lady told me to tell her about my horse and I did, I told her the entire story of rescue, heart-ache, weight gain, trail rides, rain rot, everything. I poured my heart out. Showed her his tail and then she started crying with me! After about a half hour my truck returned to the front. The man came in and said normally they usually come flailing out all over the place, hooves flying every which direction, bones breaking. But not my sweet Knight. He said he slide out of that trailer as graceful as could be, folded up perfectly like a black satin sheet. It was then that I knew I did the right thing. My selfish tears of sadness and despair turned into tears of joy knowing inside that my baby wasn't suffering. He was gracefully at peace on the other side of that rainbow. On the lonely ride home with the empty trailer I realized that it wasn't even about me and doing what I could do. It wasn't about my stressful job or terrible relationships. It wasn't about my pitiful life. It was about each other and how we made it work as a team, my Knight and I. He taught me a lot about horse health and wellness. I'm glad that I kept him and that he didn't pass away being skinny. I understood one fact. HE, actually in turn, rescued ME. I had a bracelet made from his tail and sent it to

Kelly as a thank-you for saving OUR lives. Couple years later I was finally able to afford to have a memory shadow box made, complete with his halter, shoe and the rest of his tail. It's beauti-

Carrie Emerson-Boyd

ful!

THE LION HORSE

Submitted by MARK H.

W hen I was in my twenties, I was an adventurer. I traveled the world and have had some amazing adventures! When I was in Africa, I was traveling in a very remote region with my mates. We were staying at a village who had been plagued by a lion killing their goats. We had been there a couple of weeks and were trying to help them build a wall of sorts to keep the lions out of the goat area.

We all thought it was working until another goat was killed. There was nothing else we could do for them and we had to move on with our travels. So we said our goodbyes and set out on our adventures.

About 2 months later, we were back in the region and decided to stay at the village again. Upon our arrival, we were greeted like long lost friends. We noticed they had even less goats then before, and saw there was a horse tied out in a clearing, all skin and bones and looked about to drop.

I inquired about the horse and was told that it was a trap for the lion. When she came for the horse, they would attack it and kill. I asked if they thought they would be able to get to it before it killed the horse. I was told that they were going to sacrifice the horse to get the lion!

This poor mare had lost all hopes of living, and you could see it in her sad face and eyes, and the way she just hung her head.

I couldn't deal with this, thinking of my own horse back home. I proceeded to get on my SAT Phone, and called rangers. I was able to get them to agree to come and help the village!

A week later the rangers showed and were actually able to trap and relocate the lion! The poor horse, well, I had been spending a lot of time with her, bringing her food and water, and just sitting with her. I of course had gotten attached, and didn't know what to do for her when I was leaving the village. I spoke with the elders, and was granted permission to keep the horse.

Ok, I am in a strange country, and have been given a horse. What am I going to do? Well, it is a good thing I have a friend who

lives there and runs a sanctuary! He agreed to take the horse and give her a great forever home. When he sent a transport for us- horse

included- we were able to get her to a vet. She was only 2 years old, and a body score of 1.

This was several years ago, and to this day my friend still has her, and she is in amazing shape, and treated like her new name- a QUEEN!

MEJORADO

Submitted by JACKIE

Meet Mejorado, or May. Aged crossbred gelding I found on the Moores Equines for Rescue Facebook page. I saw his photo and immediately fell in love. I was looking for something young and spunky, a project, but as soon as I saw him I knew he was the one.

His eyes, filled with sadness and confusion, he had no hope, but they were also gentle, and kind. I begged my mother for days, I couldn't take him off my mind. She finally agreed to buy him for me.

He was shipped to quarantine, and the photos when he first got to quarantine were awful. He was so thin and malnourished. 2 weeks into quarantine I went to meet him. As soon as I got to his stall I wrapped him in a giant hug, and he wrapped his neck around my body, embracing me. He had gained so much weight already, and there was beginning to be a small light in his eye. I brushed him for hours before I mounted him. He stood as I mounted him. Using a halter and paracord reins, and no saddle. He was more sensitive to my aids than any horse I've ridden. I walked and did a tiny bit of trot. The whole ride was about 10 minutes, and after I was done, the light in his eye had grown even bigger. He had figured out that I was his new mom. That he was safe forever. I brushed him for several more hours, while he grazed. I untangled his mane, which has become basically one giant knot, and fed him some cookies.   When it was time for me to leave, and he was in his stall, I embraced him one more time. As he wrapped me in his long, thin neck, I told him he would never be hungry, or hurt again, he would be home soon.

2 weeks later he finally got home. I stayed at the barn until almost 10 at night waiting. The first thing he did when he arrived was nicker at me, and wrap his neck around me. Over the weeks he became stronger, and gained weight. He would go English, western, dressage, would jump anything, but most importantly, he took care of anyone who was on his back. There was one time I was riding

him bareback in a halter, and I decided to jump a 2'9"-3' vertical. He cleared it easily, but I began to slip to the side. He slowly halted, and raised his shoulder a little, which put me back in the middle. Countless times he saved me from falling. After a couple of months we moved

barns. The new barn had tons of kids, and a huge field we could gallop in. I allowed the owner to use him in a few lessons a week, and eventually sold him to her, with a contract, and I still saw him at least a few times a week.

Everyone who rode him adored May. He taught many kids to canter and jump, and took care of the older riders. One woman in particular. There was a 79 year old woman who had emphysema and only ever rode one horse at the barn, but due to an injury the horse was laid up for a few weeks, so they had her ride May. The woman had not trotted more than half of one long side in 2 years, so when the trainer said she could ask May to trot, he lifted his feet up more, so she would feel like she was trotting. However later in the lesson, she asked again, may trotted this time, as he could feel she was more comfortable at this point, and she was able to trot almost a full lap. This woman rode him every week from that point on, and would spend 3 hours every Friday just grooming him.

May also developed a very strong bond with a young thoroughbred named Truman, and when Truman left the farm, he and an older, blind Appaloosa named Nick became inseparable.

May was put to sleep July 12, 2018, due to an abscess that became infected and did not respond to antibiotics, causing him great pain. Nick was laid to rest the same day due to a fall that broke his leg. May was 33 and Nick was in his late 30's when they were laid to rest together. May changed so many people's lives and taught me so much over the 2 1/2 years I knew him. He changed my life, and was easily the best horse I've ever had.

PENNY

Submitted by STACY

She was a kids pony, once upon a time. She had been a trusted companion and had taken grate care of her riders, carrying them through the hills and ponds,to the show ring, even pulling a little cart. But as time wore on, and the kids grew, she was forgotten. Left alone in a pasture with cattle. 30 years passed and now she was old and grey. She had seen the cattle coming and going for all those years, but never saw a human come to give her a brushing or a pet.

She was a registered gaited sheltand pony, and it was such a shame that she had taken her kids to the show ring, and had won many ribbons for them, but ended up discarded.

Though I will never know the rest of the story, this is how

we met.

I went to the auction to just look. I saw this shaggy old looking pony running through loose with a group of full size horses. Her head was down and she looked ready to drop. I did not bid on her, and regret it to this day. But the man who did buy her paid a whopping $30. I know this man and know he is a slaughter buyer. Throughout the auction, this kept nagging at me. I didn't know anything about this pony but just knew she didn't deserve this!

I went outside and found his rig, Loaded with horses and one small pony at the very back of the trailer. I found the man and begged him to let me buy her. He told me for him to unload her it would be $250! I did not argue, handing over the cash.

She came right off the trailer and I could see just how bad of a shape she was in. I loaded her into my rig and took her straight home.

The next day she had a full work up at the vet, where he said she had to be ancient because she doesn't have any top teeth! And very few lowers! I figured she probably didn't have long to be on this earth,but I would make it the best ever! A week later, I received her papers in the mail! Complete with last owners info! I contacted the man listed and was told that he had bought her about 40 years ago for

his kids, and proceeded to tell me her whole story! He even sent me a few picture of her when his kids were riding her 30 years ago!

So here it is 3 years later and she is living life to the full-lest- as much as an ancient pony can! But she eats fine, gets her pedicures regularly, and is completely loved!

PHOENIX

Submitted by CHRISSY

I t all began one evening over looking a golf course turned pasture out side of a little town called Labelle. There used to be a restaurant in the Oxbow hotel and Joe and I would sit at the window over looking the cows, this skinny young horse and the alligators in the water.

This horse would chase the cows biting them and was mean to them. I asked the one waitress , who's horse is that? She replied no one's. She began telling me the heart breaking story of this young colt.

A man had brought a bunch of horses in for a local rodeo that came from Brazil, this man's home country. He used the horses for what ever they did with them and then rounded them up to take to slaughter. This skinny young horse who by now I found out was just 6 months old was born in the pasture. His mom and he were rounded up and put into a trailer to go to slaughter but this young colt escaped and ran for his life. These men tried to catch him but he was to quick and out smarted them each time.The men finally were tired and gave up. They closed up the trailer and pulled out. This colt was screaming for his mom and mom was screaming back for her baby but the truck just rolled on. This young horse ran aside the fence desperately trying to get back to him mom but the truck turned the corner on to the highway and was soon out of sight.

The colt ran and slipped down an embankment into the canal filled with alligators and swam across it to the adjoining pasture trying to find his mother. He cried out for her but she could no longer hear him as the truck was to far down the road and this would be the last time the two would ever see or be with each other again for life.This 6 month old colt now had to fend for him self with no protection from predators in a huge empty field. He managed to get by on the grasses of summer and a pond for water.

Joe said to me one evening while watching him, you wanted a horse for a long time, why don't you have him captured and trained? I said I'm 53 and a bit old to be starting out with a baby. He said look at

him, he needs you. I started going to the feed store and buying sweet feed and a bale of hay I'd keep in the trunk of my car and each

evening I'd go out and sit on the gate and call him by the only name I'd known" Oxbow".
I'd call out Oxbow, come get your supper. It didn't take long for him to come running when he heard my voice but I knew I was just the waitress bring him his dinner. After he'd gobble down all the sweet feed he no longer wanted to be around me but I hung in there and continued to go out thinking perhaps we could become friends.

I was terrified to get in the pasture with him as I didn't know any thing about horses and had no clue what he was trying to tell me. I think he sensed my fear and perhaps he also had trust issues from his mom being taken away.

Where I lived there was an elder women named Miss Betty who sold horse tack out of her garage. I stopped by one day to pick her brain and asked her for advise. She went to her garage and handed me a halter and said put this on him and you'll be ok.
I said huh? Put this on him, how? She said get in the pasture and show no fear, horses can sense that you know. I told her I was afraid of him. She assured me all would be ok and to watch his eyes and ears and taught me how to read them to know what he was going to do and what he was thinking.

I went out to the pasture with carrots as a peace offering and called him. Through the tall grasses came movement and soon he popped his head through and came trotting up. He never got to close to pet but we were building that bridge of trust ever so slowly.

I hopped over the gate but stayed right at it coaxing him to come in for the carrots as he was food driven. He came in and I listened to Miss Betty about the eyes and ears. I approached him directly head on and he wasn't having any of that. He taunted me and avoided me or getting close to me to try to put his halter on. After hours or trying and carrots gone I headed him.

The next day I came back and tried again and went further into the pasture. I was shaking so back I thought I'd cause an earthquake

lol. I finally managed to get it on him with a very loose fit. He ran off

with it on and fear struck my heart, oh no what if he got caught on some thing, he could break his neck or die.

I got up early the following morning and went back out and when Oxbow came back he still had the halter on. I said whew. I tired to get it off but he learned quickly and wouldn't come in to me. On the third day I went out and it was off of his face and gone. I felt a sigh of relief. I stopped by Miss Betty's and told her about getting the halter on and he took it off. She laughed and said that's a smart horse!

I kissed a lot of dirt from him and he was unpredictable. We hung in there together, worked through the bad and embraced the good. To this day were still working through the bad and focusing on the positive. Phoenix still treats me like I'm the waitress bring his dinner and I think many horse people experience that.

We are a work in progress and just take it day to day. We've had at least 8 trainers to date , most worked him once or twice and said they'd never come back. Sigh so it's back to RFDTV and video's from horse trainers.

Phoenix and I were invited by a woman named Carrie to a clinic she was hostessing. I was so excited !! Phoenix and I had never gone to a clinic. Carrie came to the barn I was at and loaded him and we took him over night to her facility. That evening Phoenix had a private session with the trainer. He did amazing for the trainer and the trainer taught me a lot. Everyone that came the next day loved Phoenix and one lady said name your price lol. I said he's not for sale but thank you. Phoenix and I learn together and some times it doesn't work so I ask him how should I do this and he shows me. We've come a long way and have miles and miles to go but were doing it together. Where many said get rid of that horse before he kills you, I dig in deeper and said I made a deal with him when I captured him we'd stick it out and that's what I'm going to do.

On bad day's he for sale right now, on good day's he's mine for ever.

I had a DNA test done on him and he came back as a 1st marker

Mangalarga Marchador which is the official horse of Brazil, 2nd marker Shetland pony , third marker Norwegian Fjord. Since his mom was Brazilian the first marker makes sense. These horses are very rare in the US. There is no draft in Phoenix that I can see, he's a smaller horse.

Phoenix and I are making strides and some days can be a challenge and other day's he's a sweetheart. Phoenix is now 8 years old and we've been together 7 years. I suspect we'll be together until the end. A promise is a promise.

RAY

Submitted by CHYNNA

Hi there my name is Chynna and I live in Farmington, Ct. I am 24 years old and currently struggle with the lasting effects from a TBI. Horses have always brought me joy and helped me cope with my struggles .As they could be way worse, daily headaches,PTSD, and anxiety depression are some. Seeing my horse everyday soothes those dilemmas I have, and can even calm my anxiety greatly.

I had been an avid rider most of my life. Although it wasn't until I turned 18 that I really started showing and jumping. Lots of fun, but I found myself loving the caring for, teaching and companionship of my horses that really made me happy. Horses had pulled me out of a deep dark place and that was when I met my heart horse. Raisin The Barr aka RayRay.

I rescued Ray in 2016. He was no foal no more! He was a 16 hand 6 year old love bug! He originally was rescued by Ray of Light Farm in East Haddam, Ct just months old in 2010. He learned the basics at Ray of Light and some under saddle work until he was ready for adoption. He was the first horse I met in the barn and the one I couldn't stop thinking about in between visits. I spent my summer there in 2016 riding and working with Raisin. Until in September 2016 I was given the opportunity to adopt him. Of course i said yes!

Come that day he loaded like a champ, and when he got home he had no idea what to do besides go meet his friends. Minnie a rescued Percheron mare and Tucker a rescued Halflinger who is the same age as Ray.

Raisin and I rode around the property and hung out for a while. We eventually went to the Portland Fair about a month into his move and I couldn't have been more proud. He took my anxious, very scared self around those rings like he had been doing it his whole life. My heart grew even larger.

We have had a few vet visits over the years. Some very interesting ones and the usual check ups. One visit being because "Raisin ate almost a bag of shavings" We couldn't figure out what he was thinking. He had managed to pull the bag off the loft about his shed. So I continuously hang dog toys along his shed wall to keep his lips busy. Well it was working for a while, Until i saw him eating dirt and rocks. The poor guy had an ulcer we concluded. 4 weeks of gastroguard good to go!

Oh! We had found a wolf tooth on our first teeth exam. I felt so bad for him when they were pulling it out. But boy was that a big tooth!!

Due to the poor breeding of PMU's he has a very very thick set of cheeks and lips. As he grew they have gotten thicker and has made bridling a battle. So we ride around in a halter and lead rope. Still fun.

Speed up to current day, Raisin had come in from the field

one night with a swollen eye and forehead then began to swell days following along with his tail becoming stuck to the side and had then failed his neurological exam. Blood test was positive for EPM. We have kept our heads up and hung out more than ever and have seen extreme progress. We have been treating for EPM 2 months now and could not be happier. We have another month of treatment and I bet we are golden.

Raisin and I are best friends. We keep each other happy. I love sitting in his stall with him late at night. Those full moon nights, listening to him munch his hay are priceless sounds. He is the only horse I know that when he plays all four hooves jump off the ground in enthusiasm or comes galloping when I call him. Or who likes a radio on 24/7 locked in his shed or not. He walks right next to me when I'm walking, stops when I stop and will even run the fence line with me. It is so much fun! He has come to sharing his breakfast each morning with his three girlfriends, they're goats. Bravo, Trifecta, and Aspen. He is the laziest quarter horse, Thoroughbred, Draft cross I have ever met and would never change a thing for the world.

Raisin currently lives on my family's farm in Harwinton-,Ct. Still with his friends Minnie and Tucker and girlfriends too.

STONEY

Submitted by LESLIE

I met Stoney by chance. I wasn't looking for him, but he found me.

My son was wanting a 2 year old to train, so I told him we would go pick up a cheap one at the kill pen. That way, if he messed her up terribly, she would still be better off than if she went to the killers!

I tried to put on my blinders and just focus on the pen full of 2 years olds I had to choose from. But for one instant, I glanced up. I saw the saddest eyes I had ever seen. He was begging me to save him. I couldn't look away. I absolutely could not afford to get two horses, so out came the credit card.

Stoney, as I soon named him, was just under 16 hands, buckskin paint, and at least 300 pounds underweight. He wasn't pretty. But his eyes, I couldn't walk away.

After about a week of good food, medical care, and bonding time, I decided to ride him. It didn't take long to figure out how he ended up in a kill pen. He was extremely head shy. It was obvious he had taken some hits to the head. He was fine in the pen, but when I rode him out, he would spin around and try to head back to the barn. When I said "no", he fought harder and reared. Since I am the most stubborn person alive, I won the debate. It only took three rides and that issue was done.

Enter Kevin the farrier. Let me preface by saying I have a fantastic farrier. He is calm and gentle and really works with the horses. Stoney assumed he was Satan incarnate. Stoney would rear up and try to pull his feet away, a look of sheer panic on his face. Kevin was so wonderful and patient with him. After about three visits, Stoney was completely at ease and there was no fight in him.

The most amazing thing about him came to me as an accidental discovery. A friend of mine was riding him while I was riding my other horse. We were having a nice little ride down a dirt road when a deer jumped up in the trees beside us. We all jumped! My friend lost her balance and was about to fall. Stoney moved his body up under her

and helped her regain her balance. I thought it was a fluke. I was wrong.

Another time I was riding him and ponying a colt. The colt spooked and managed to jump around behind Stoney, wrapping me up in the rope. Stoney flipped his body around, untangling me and getting me out of danger.

Another time, I kicked Stoney into a lope. He did a little celebratory kick up and I lost my balance. He again moved his body under me and got me balanced.

Later I was riding and had a blood sugar crash. We were a couple of miles from home and I had no choice but to stay on and ride back to the barn. Again, Stoney knew I was in trouble. He slowed at ever dip in the ground and careful placed each foot as to not dislodge me. I just sat there and her carefully carried me safely back home.

Stoney was never in my plan. I wasn't looking for a big, ugly headed, mischievous gelding. But he was looking for me. We are so bonded now. I have been told, "That horse would do cartwheels for you if you asked." I certainly know I would do them for him.

TOBY'S STORY

Submitted by Jahar L.

I am from a small country that believes in using horses as a tool. We do not look at them as pets or companions. We use them for transportation, and sometimes meals.

One day, I was riding my horse down a lane, and saw a foal, no more than a couple of hours old lying in a ditch, covered in mud. I hopped off my old mare and went to check on the foal. He was barely alive, and filthy. I knew I could not leave him there, covered in flies and ants, so I scooped him up and put him over my horse to take him home.

Once there, I milked our goat, and began trying to get him to take the bottle. After an hour of trying, and about ready to give up, he did it!

He was a little champ about it! Every day he grew

stronger. In the meantime, I had found out that the foal belonged to a man who we all knew has no heart when it comes to animals. His mare had foaled while out making deliveries, and as soon as she did, he harnessed her back up and drove her off. He did not need a baby slowing him down.

Fast forward to 6 months later, and now I have a healthy, happy colt! He goes everywhere with me. I do not look at him or any other horse as a tool, and I never have! This little guy is my shadow! He follows me to market, school, and on fun walks!

Now here we are 3 years later, and I broke him myself, and am riding him every day! He is a beautiful solid black stallion, and gentle as a puppy!

The man who had abandoned him on the side of the road has found out about him, and demanded his return. Saying it is his property! He demands I either return him or pay for him! I do not have any money as we only have a small farm and no money for extras.

The village heard of this and came together to pool enough money to save this little colt from the horrible man who wanted this horse as a servant. This man has killed more horses than anyone in

our village has ever had! And everyone knew of this gentle colt and knew how I had gotten him! They had a meeting and offered the man

the money they had put together to save the colt. The man refused
the money. I was in tears. I was a 10 year old who had saved this horse alone, and couldn't stand the thought of losing him!

I don't know what happened next, I was told to wait outside of the meeting. But when that man came outside, he gave me a look that chilled me to the core. But the elder cam over to me and handed me a slip of paper. It was a BILL of Ownership! Somehow, they had convinced him to sell me the colt!

I had that colt until he passed away of old age. Still Miss

him!

XANDER'S STORY

Submitted by SHERRIE

My daughter and I bought an OTTB two years ago from a horse trader. Originally we just wanted to save him from his current situation. We found out later that his first off track adopter loved him but didn't think he would be able to compete. She thought she had found a great home for him. The horse trader she gave Xander to portrayed themselves as providing a forever family home. The horse trader did not intentionally neglect Xander. They were not knowledge-able about how to care for a fresh OTTB and he lost so much weight that he was skeletal when we got him. On top of that they trimmed his feet to the point they bled and he could barely walk. On the trailer ride home I drove 30 miles an hour and ar-ranged to have my vet meet me at the farm. The first few days we the worst. We didn't know if he would live. Did I mention I paid

900.00 for him!

It didn't matter. He needed help and he touched our hearts. Once he was out of the woods, I started researching him. I had no papers, but I had the nagging feeling I had seen him before. With luck I found his old ad from his first adopter. She gave me his registered name and was very happy to hear he was safe.

We had no expectations that a lame roach backed horse would do much but he has surprised us all!
He was a successful racehorse. He even had a fan page at one time.
He is now on his way to being a successful eventer. My daughter is just starting out so he has only done some schooling shows and pony club meetings but he is a star every time he steps into the arena. He is gentle enough to allow beginners to learn off him but he is bold enough to fly around a 2' 9" to 3' course. Oh and he moves beautifully when asked. His roach back has almost disappeared. He is sound

and strong. We love him dearly as he is truly one in a million, that unicorn everyone wants. We have had multiple offers from

professional equestrians that would love to buy him, but He is home He is family, and he is NOT for sale.

Carrie Emerson-Boyd

ZINNIA'S STORY

Submitted by AMBER

T his is Zinnia's story and the story of a horse that was in the most critical state of starvation I have ever seen. One that was severely emaciated to the point the vet said she had a small chance of survival and one that when I first laid my eyes on her absolutely broke my heart. But let me start from the beginning.

Hurricane Harvey hit the South Texas in August of 2017 and my husband and I felt called to help rescue horses and livestock that were left behind in the massive flooding. On our 4th day, we were down in the Beaumont/Katy/areas assisting with horse rescue (and a couple cows) from the flood waters and we were getting low on supplies, so we were getting ready to head back to Austin. Anyway it was about 9pm at night and I got a call from Jennifer Williams (director of BEHS) asking me if we could pick up an emergency seizure. So we ended up staying another night so we could pick up the horse.

We met the local sheriff at the house where Zinnia was and he told me, I don't know if this horse is going to make the ride up to Austin. When I first saw her my heart sank. I felt absolutely devastated for this poor sweet horse. As you can see Zinnia was experiencing severe starvation, was in poor shape, could barely walk and she had been standing in a mud pit for almost a week. She had open wounds on her legs where her skin was sloughing off and she also had severe rain rot on her back.

She also had a hard time walking because her muscles were so depleted. After we loaded her in my trailer, we took her immediately to the vet that was working at Montgomery County Fair grounds. The vet examined her and said she only had a 50% chance of survival

because of how bad her starvation was and he didn't think she could make the trailer ride up to my house in Georgetown (outside of Austin). He gave her some antibiotics then the fairgrounds and would

not offer to hold her because of how bad her starvation. We ended up taking Zinnia to Denise Crosthwaits' (BEHS Foster Coordinator) house in College Station (about 45 minutes away from the fairgrounds). After we had dropped Zinnia off at Denise's all we could think about was how much she needed a loving home and how heartbreaking her situation was. On our drive back to Georgetown we decided we wanted to adopt her and see her through her recovery and give her a forever retirement home.

She is about 20yo. Anyway, Denise and her husband got Zinnia the immediate care she needed from their vet and they also cared for her wounds and skin loss on her legs. After two weeks of intensive care at Denise's house Zinnia was ready to travel so I went and picked her up and brought her home. It took us a few months for all the rain rot to go away, and a few more weeks of wound care to get her wounds on her legs to heal. It took 7 months for her to recover from the starvation and get back to good health. During that recovery, she won our hearts through her sweet, gently disposition and she will have a forever home with us for the remainder of her life.

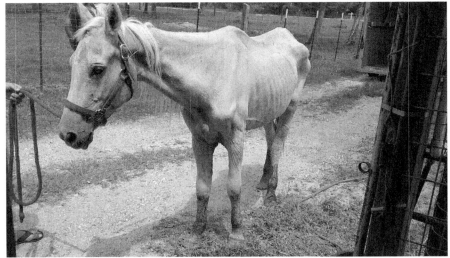

◆ ◆ ◆

THE HUNTSMAN'S HORSE

Submitted by LAUREN

◆ ◆ ◆

I rescued an OTTB from a farm where he was being fed minimal hay and little to no grain. I have had him for a year and a half and he has gained almost 300 pounds. He is now a huntsman's horse for Commonwealth Foxhounds in Westmoreland County and he does hunters on the off season. He's gone from not knowing what a ring or leads meant, to jumping a 3' course with ease. He has the biggest puppy dog personality and loves teaching my younger lesson kids.

Another pony I rescued where the owner admitted he didn't have the funds to take care of him and told me if I had the means to, he could be mine. So I brought him home as a scrawny 5 year old who only weighed 500 pounds and beefed him up to a stout almost 900 pounds in a matter of months. He had never been backed before, and he was the easiest ever. Another huge personality in a small body. He also foxhunts, does cross country, jumps 3' courses with ease, and everyone who has met him has fallen in love. I sold him last year, as a 9 year old, to a young girl who wanted a pony club mount, and they both have blossomed together.

◆ ◆ ◆

GRACIBELLE

Submitted by MELINDA

My husband purchased me a sweet Mare in may of 2018 from Sextons Horse & mule co. She was just a little shy and a tad bit under weight and had a cold. I called my vet out right away as I wanted the best for my sweet girl.

My husband has a gelding that I am terrified of, and when Miss Gracie came off of the trailer it was love at first site, I knew she was mine.

Being from the city I have never been around horses nor have I ever ridden, so therefore I am as green as they come. I even asked how pork and beans where grew in the garden when I first moved in with my husband, lol.   Finally the day came that I was gonna try and ride Gracie as they said she was ready to ride, I was so nervous I am sure she felt it herself, but she took me for a ride like I was a pro, while my husband stood back and laughed at me. Why did he laugh at me? Because instead of me clicking her with my heels at the time to make her go I just picked her reins up and said "Giddy Up Gracie Lets go" and she went.

My husband and the farrier said she did really good to put up with someone as green as me. She really is a blessing and a sweet horse and I am not afraid to be around her . I do not do shows or nothing fancy just ride and love her here at home on my property where its safe. She could not be a better fit for me, when we purchased her she was fixing to go on truck to go to slaughter.

She has a happy home now and is very loved and spoiled too. Oh yeah she also has her a boyfriend too! Her favorite treats are carrots and a bite of country ham biscuit minus the ham from the local store and it makes her smile at the sun and look for more!

LITTLE JOHN

Submitted by RICHARD

L ittle John" August 19, 2017. I received a phone call from
my girlfriend, Pazia Kennedy. "I'm bringing a horse
home," she said. "A girl on the drill team got him with
another horse, but she doesn't want him to die on her...... So we
wondered if you could try to help him." I thought to myself that
it couldn't really be that bad, the girls were probably exaggerat-
ing a little bit. So I told her to bring him on home and we'd see.

It was a decision that drastically changed my life! A
couple of hours later, I met "Little John" for the first time. Back-
ing in the driveway, she got out and I met her at the trailer. "He's
so skinny and pitiful, I don't know if he'll make it", she told me.
I opened the trailer to see one of the saddest things that I've

ever seen before in my life. Little John was nothing but skin and bones. You could see that he had been a really big horse at one time, but he was so skinny and barely standing up in the trailer. We tried to coax him to back out of the trailer, but he just quivered and couldn't seem to move. I wasn't sure this wasn't going to end sooner rather than later. But I'm a hard headed fella, and don't give up easily. I'm a big guy, 6'6 and 270 pounds, but I wasn't sure if I could hold him up or not, even as skinny as he was.

So we finally got him out, with me physically holding him up. When he finally lurched out of the trailer, I thought that we were both going down. But we stayed upright, and rested for a moment or two. It couldn't have been more than 40 or 50 feet from the trailer to cross the road to the pasture gate, but it took us forever to get him to limp over there, with me holding him up the whole way. Once we were back in the grass, he stayed upright without me holding him. He sniffed and checked the grass out like he didn't know what it was. We later learned that the people who gave him up admitted to leaving him in a dry lot without feeding him for a YEAR!!!! He was a big guy, standing around 16-3 to 17 hands, but probably only weighed 7 or 800 pounds. I would swear that if the sun was right, you could see through

the poor old horse. Things didn't look good.   Little John showed brands from the Arkansas Prison horse system, so we looked up the brand to determine that he was the first colt born in 1992. So, at this point, he was 25 years old. Things just kept stacking up against the poor guy. Picking up his hooves showed him to be so malnourished that you could take your thumbs and leave indention's in his hoof. I didn't have much hope at this point. 25 years old, starved to nothing, feet so tender he could barely move......... was it even worth trying? I was determined to give it a go. He was ALWAYS hungry, but couldn't eat very much at first. I was scared we'd kill him WITH food. I also worried about him staying hydrated, as he couldn't hardly move more than a few feet without just giving up.

I contacted our equine vet, Dr. Angel Jordan, and we got together to look him over and come up with a game plan. Vaccinations and worming were high on the list. Then a program to build him up. Would it work? Luckily for John, she found little wrong with him other than being starved. So we started soaking beet pulp and mixing it with a high fat feed. He got tiny portions several times a day, gradually increasing the amount of food and decreasing the number of feedings. For a while we mixed a little Bute in his food for the discomfort. This ending up upsetting his stomach, so we added a little liquid aloe vera in to help with that. His feet remained an issue, as they were so soft, cracked, and split up the hoof walls. Anything that got in his frog would pretty much cripple him.

So once a day, I'd clean his hooves and soak them for a few minutes in a pie pan with a little turpentine in it. This helped to harden them up. He was still in poor condition when the wagon races came up, so I drove home from Clinton every day to take care of him and make sure that he was doing as well as possible. I'm sure people thought that I was foolish for taking so much time to try and help a 25 year old horse! I kept getting the "he's not gonna make it", or, "he'll never be worth anything again". I wasn't worried about that. The old

horse had stolen a little piece of my heart, and I would do anything possible to make what was left of his life great.

We made our way up to 2 pounds of beet pulp and 6 pounds of high fat feed twice a day.......... so 16 pounds a day. All the hay and grass that he could eat. And water..... I'm not sure how much he drank, and how much he slung out of the tub playing in it, but getting down to the pond edge was tough on him, so I filled an old bath tub for him daily. If it wasn't filled quickly enough, he'd stand next to it and mope. Feeding Little

John was like throwing hundred dollar bills out the window at high speed. I think that we figured once that he ate more in a week than all the other seven put together. But gradually, he got a little bit better.   One morning I went to the gate to feed him and called for him. He wasn't up at the gate like normal, and I was concerned. So I hollered out for him, and the next thing that I knew, I could hear a thundering of hooves that sounded like Oaklawn..... Little John came in wide open!!!!!! He's got a soft lil purring sound that he makes, and it was almost like he was laughing. John was getting better!

Sometime around late October, we were given an OTTB named Zen that we put out in the pasture with John. They became fast friends. Given that they both stand around 16-3 or 17 hands, they made a pretty pair anyways. Winter came and went, and John showed us another side of himself. Two litters of puppies were born to strays in our hay barn, and he stood calmly and patiently watching over them. If Zen strayed closer than he liked, he'd stand in between them. He wintered well, still eating everything that came by. As spring rolled around, John was feeling his oats. We've seen him rear up to his full height on his back feet, then take off running and bucking. We were able to capture video of him and Zen playing in the pond. Careful trimming and lots of maintenance on his hooves had really brought him a long ways. Now 26 years old, John is probably the most playful and rambunctious horse that we own! He's had his year of rest, to make up for the bad times, and now it's time to get ready to ride a little bit!

TEGAN

Submitted by DEBBIE

My name is Debbie. My husband and I own a small farm in Mt Airy MD. While there have been numerous rescues that have come to call our place home, this is the story of a special one!

I was looking for a horse for my husband. He is not the horse lover, it's me. He's a big guy, 6' tall. He loves carriages and buggies and a year prior had bought an old buggy on a whim at an estimate auction (Again, he's not the horse person. Lol) He is fascinated with the old buggies and carriages tho. And had expressed interest in wanting to ride also, just needing a "quiet one with brakes"

We went to the auction in Pa several times just didn't see "his horse" Although I did come home with the cutest pony ever one of those trips, but that's another story :)

Through Facebook, a group had shared some pics and info on several horses they were able to evaluate at "the meat mans barn". He lives close to the auction and had agreed to give horses another chance to be bought before being shipped out. Yes he's a known buyer and his barn is packed full, the tractor and trailer sitting out in front ready to roll!

So back to my story. A couple of pictures and a short video were shared of an older beat up Amish work horse. She was ridden bareback, had harness scars new and old, and in the one photo that I can't seem to locate, I knew she was the one! In a barn packed full of horses who had given in. All their heads hanging down in defeat, there she was, head up, ears perked forward, peeking out of a small window in his barn, knowing it was not her time!

Plans were made, and I was there 2 days later, 3 hours away, picking her up! It was a trip I will never forget! That barn had every bit of 100 horses in there, in various pens. They were all quiet for the most part. There WAS auto waters and excellent hay around for all! I don't blame him, he's a part of the horrible process. He isn't the one who used her, neglected her and sent her to auction. He was honestly ok dealing with directly, and I didn't feel the $100 above what he paid for her was outrageous. He did take his time to go to the auction,
purchase and haul her to his place. He did allow her a second chance. But, the truck sat out front hooked to the trailer. There is NO DOUNT

where she would have gone.

In Oct. 2017 I brought home #816. The very next day she became Tegean. (Welsh origin meaning pretty girl, loved one, darling). My husband kept talking to her and calling her pretty girl. She didn't know what a treat or carrot was. She was terrified of fly spray and the spray of hoses. But, she has been since day one of her new life, sweet, kind and grateful. She is everything my husband needed and everything I didn't know I needed. She had 6 months off to rest, become just a horse again, and learn to trust us. She didn't even really know how to socialize w the other horses here, it all took time. She was a loner ever after her quarantine. A little over a year now, and Tegean is home forever!

She has a boyfriend, perfect stall manners, she will stand tied up all day, she walks right on the trailer, she loves trail rides and rides in our ring w kids! She never cared about a bareback ride or my husband and his saddle and his nerves. She gave him the confidence he needed! She was just this month harnesses up for the first time in our barn in a cold and wet day, and handled it like the pro she is. It was a loaner harness, we will be ordering her her own custom set w only her comfort in mind, as we slowly pursue an occasion buggy ride with her. She will never have to work in the field again, or know hunger or ill fitting equipment.

She isn't the first rescue here, and she probably isn't the last, but Tegean has filled a big mans heart with the love and confidence in horses he was wanting. She IS what "Rescue" stands for in every sense of the word. To us, she is perfect, all $325 of her!!

Tegean is now 19 yrs old, they were even accurate in estimating her age.

She lives w her bff/boyfriend Forrest here. She has most days off to do as pleases, but also eagerly leaves him to come to the barn with us

for spa days, a short ride about, or helping us learn how to "drive".

FINLEY AND TRUMAN

Submitted by KELLY

I wasn't looking for a horse when I saw Finley's picture on the Coast 2 Coast Draft Horse Rescue Facebook page. And I certainly wasn't looking for another 6 months after rescuing when I saw Truman's picture. Both came from the same kill pen in Shippensburg, PA where C2C was permitted to photograph horses and post them for purchase in an effort to keep them from shipping to Canada/Mexico to slaughter.

Finley is about 11 years old. He is a haflinger. I think he likely drove before I got him. We now ride English and western and have enjoyed natural horsemanship clinics with Greg Eliel.

Truman is retired on a Friend's farm. He is old - very old - and must have worked very hard during his life serving humans. He deserves the retirement I can give him.

From the minute I walked Finley onto my trailer I could

feel in my heart that no matter what he had endured, his heart was still open. He followed me without hesitation onto my trailer. It was a freezing mid-January day on the top of a small mountain in PA. It had just started to snow. The wind was howling. And this horse that I had only just laid eyes on was willing to trust me.

Many hours of white knuckle driving later he followed me off the trailer and into a strange barn without missing a step. The next morning he looked over the stall as though he awaited our next adventure. My first ride was down a road to the ocean. Finley stopped and stared in amazement but trusted me and together we went forward down the beach. In hindsight I wonder if he had ever been ridden. It wouldn't surprise me if he only drove in his past but true to himself he trusted me enough to let me mount up.

Finley has been trail riding with me, gone to high end English barns for lessons and has impressed natural horsemanship trainer Greg Eliel with his heart and willingness to try. His fear is ever present but his willingness to still trust prevails.

Truman is the polar opposite. Truman is much, much older and shows signs of a lot of hard work and not a lot of kindness.

Truman took over an hour to load and only did so backward up the ramp, too afraid to face what could be next for him. Truman would not move toward his grain or hay for weeks until the person feeding him backed away but showed kindness and comfort with our goats and donkeys. Truman was terrified of confinement and it got to the point where he was allowed to wander loose on our property. Truman now lives on a friends farm in upstate NY where he has hundreds of acres and a huge run in. He doesn't have to be confined, fear people or work. He just has to try to heal from whatever taught him to carry so much fear. When I visit Truman and he lets me pet him and give me carrots he reminds me that scars run deep and some never heal. He reminds me that his past is always with him and he compels me to try to show kindness, have a soft hand and a re-assuring voice for those who need comfort to cope with their pain.

AURORA

Submitted by NIKKI

W e are called the Santana Center, located in Rhode Island. Here is a cute story about one of our horses Aurora, who was adopted by a wonderful woman named Diane.

It was December in Rhode Island and 17 degrees – a sharp contrast to warm & sunny LA where I'd flown in from a week before. We'd just lost my Stepdad, and Mom needed help.

I took a temp job grooming horses at a boarding barn and riding school. When Aurora's brown eyes locked on me from inside her dank, dark, frozen stall she'd been swaying and cribbing in for days on end, they pleaded "Get me OUT OF HERE! NOW!" I looked around. Surely that was meant for someone else. "Me?" I answered. "You talking to ME?" She snorted, then continued swaying. She was so thin. Her hooves were overgrown. Her coat was black and dull. Ms.LeanMean, the manager of that 50 horse barn, walked over to me and warned, "Don't go near HER – she'll tear your arm off. I'm supposed to drive her to some sanctuary in New Hampshire. What a pain in the ass. I wish she'd just DIE! Save me the trouble. Ya WANT her? She's FREE." Aurora WOULD die if she stayed there. She belonged in a field of wildflowers, swooshing her tail and frolicking like all happy horses do.

For days I finished feeding and grooming the others early enough to spend a few hours walking, brushing, spoiling Aurora with extra hay I'd steal for her. She'd dip it in water to soften it before chewing. Wasn't she clever? I covered her with a blanket so she'd stop shivering. She loved carrots. Hated apples. Spit them right out! I called old high-school friends. "Ya know anyone who'll foster her til I can find a forever home?" No luck. The other groomers whispered snippets of stories to me: She was a racehorse, then a blue-ribbon winning jumper/hunter, abruptly dumped by her owner – a career equestrian who ran off with boyfriend #2, leaving Aurora behind with rich boyfriend #1, who kept her outside for 5 years before he got fed up and brought her there 2 months earlier.   The other horse that

came in with her died from a twisted gut. "We tried all night to save her. What a mess! I'm exhausted," Ms LeanMean huffed. I had to return to LA and cried myself to sleep for 7 nights straight. I made umpteen million phone calls. Finally, my stepsister, a K-9 Detective in Providence, borrowed a trailer and hauled Aurora to a farm where the Police Department boarded their horses. But Aurora was thin and unmanageable, too skiddish to work or ride. She needed vet care. "There's this woman who rehabs horses – here's her number." Well, the next thing I knew, Kathy Castro and I were blubbering together on a long distance phone call that changed Aurora's – and my – life forever.

By February The Santana Center was Aurora's home. I funneled money (donations from EVERYONE I knew) and Kathy, this compassionate, intuitive, patient, sensitive, horse loving miracle-worker, FIXED AURORA! She sent me detailed, daily progress updates with pictures! She answered all my questions. She always took my calls. Aurora was a Diva – nothing about her rehab was easy. But Kathy never gave up on her. She was determined give Aurora a sense of security.

I flew back to RI in June and drove out to The Santana Center. It was the first time I'd ever hugged a real angel. Kathy then lead me down the gravel road. And there was Aurora. I hardly recognized her. Her black, dull coat had transformed to a beautiful, glossy, light mahogany. Her tail swooshed! Her stomach was round, and there was even a bit of muscle showing from her daily exercise routine. Kathy was riding her and Aurora was loving it! She was a whole new gal, standing there calmly IN A FIELD OF WILDFLOWERS! She snorted at me. That day, we 3 spent hours together. It felt dreamlike. I returned to L.A. Months went by. Aurora grew stronger, healthier, more trusting. By November, Kathy and I decided Aurora was ready to move on. We tried finding her a home in Rhode Island, but Kathy was sure Aurora

belonged with me and encouraged me to take her. We found a transport company, and Aurora, by then sound in body & mind, made a 5 day cross-country trek, to spend her next 7 years in the California sun. Kathy counseled me all the way. Aurora lived until the ripe old age of 30. I keep her ashes in a beautiful wooden urn. I will never ever be able to repay Kathy Castro. Because of Aurora, our bond is strong, our friendship is unique and continues to this day.

Carrie Emerson-Boyd

SHADOW

Submitted by JULIE

W hen we first went to look at Shadow in February of 2006, she was wide eyed in the back of her stall. She was good for being tacked up and we tried her out and she did a good job, though we knew that there was going to be a lot of work to have her trust us.

We bought Shadow from folks who had rescued her a year before and did not have time to work with her. When we bought her, she was difficult to catch, was scared of cross ties, fly spray, going through gates, having her feet picked, and
the farrier. Even though she had problems on the ground, she was always
excellent with the kids.

One time I had taken my four year old daughter, Abigail,

with me to ride Shadow, and the gate bumped her as we were leaving the arena, and she scooted forward. Abigail's foot got stuck in the stirrup and as I was trying to get her to free her, Shadow was moving away from Abigail to keep from stepping on her. Once the stirrup came free, I let Shadow go to deal with Abigail. Once I knew that she was fine, I went and got the pony.

As I led Shadow up to Abigail, Shadow put her head in Abigail's chest to say that she was sorry. That was when we understood what a wonderful pony Shadow is.

In 2011, the kids weren't riding her much, so I taught her to drive a
cart. She eventually made the rounds of driving events in our area
doing Arena Driving Trials and Driving Derbies. She loved when we did
the driving derbies because they had a long galloping section, as the
photo depicts. We also did some recreational driving, going to local
trails that are suitable for a cart.

MIRAGE

Submitted by PAM

T he year was 1999. I was working on a farm in Cambridge, MD. My dream job. Taking care of horses and exercising them. One day a trailer load of new horses showed up. When Mirage stepped off the trailer it was love at first sight. He was only a 2 year old. Very well built. Very handsome. Beautiful bald face with piercing blue eyes. My heart skipped a beat. We were inseparable from day one. I even went to see him on my days off. He was my horsey soul mate. He was a young, green broke horse but he had an old soul. Nothing fazed him. He was wise beyond his year.

The manager of the barn had an animal communicator come in to do a reading on all of the horses. That proved to be interesting for the nonbeliever. I must admit I was a skeptic. As she read each horse she captured the spirit and essence of each horse with accuracy. She got to Mirage and asked who his person was. I stepped forward. She placed her hands on his neck and closed her eyes. She said she had done thousands of readings and has never encountered a spirit like Mirage's. He had the spirit of a very special Shaman. She finished his reading and looked at me and said "This horse is very special and never lose track of him." I smiled and thought to myself I already knew he was special.

A little over a year later the owners of the farm bought a new farm in New York. They were moving all of the horses to New York. I would have to tell my best friend good bye. I offered to buy him. He was not for sale. I told them how much I loved Mirage and if he was ever sold to please contact me.

I kissed his muzzle. I layed my face on his neck and buried my nose in his fur. I breathed in his scent and told him good bye. I looked in those striking blue eyes and told him to never forget me. I told him I would never forget him and I would always look for him. My heart was broken. He was loaded on a trailer. Good bye Mirage.

Over the years the words of the animal communicator haunted me. "Don't lose track of him." I thought of Mirage often and wondered
if he was being loved and treated well. I hoped he was happy.

15 years later on October 10, 2016, I was looking at the Horses of New Holland on Facebook like I occasionally do. I like to follow the horses that get saved and have a happy ending. The pictures of some of the horses to be auctioned were posted. I couldn't believe my eyes. It was Mirage. I knew it was him. It felt like he was looking at me through the picture.....those piercing blue eyes. My hands were shaking as I messaged the person who posted his picture.   I told her I knew the horse with hip #510. I had to find him. The New Holland auction is in Pennsylvania. I was miles away in Maryland. I felt so helpless. So far

away.

It was late afternoon when I saw his picture and Mirage was already gone. This was not over. I was not giving up. I would find him. I was at work and called my husband. "You need to get my box of old pictures and bring me every picture of Mirage." It had been 15 years since I had seen him and wanted to compare the pictures. I needed to be sure. He arrived with a handful of pictures and we layed them on the kitchen table. The horse at the auction had to be Mirage. The pictures matched up perfectly.

I shared Mirage's picture from the auction on Facebook with my plea for help in finding him. Literally within seconds it was shared dozens of times. With the help of complete strangers I was able to start getting small pieces of information. Dozens of people messaging me.

After 7 long hours and dozens of leads a name turned up. A message appeared "I think I have the horse you are looking for." I said I needed a picture of the left side of his head to be sure it was really Mirage. He has a black spot on his upper lip. By now it is a little after midnight. The next message "Give me a few minutes to get to the barn. I'm headed there now."Those were the longest 10 minutes of my life. I was shaking and my heart was racing.

Ping. A new message. The picture. When I saw the picture I broke down and started crying. Happy tears. I messaged her back. It's Mirage. Can I buy him? YES!!! So the deal was made in the wee a.m. hours and shipping was also arranged. I would be getting my boy

tomorrow afternoon.

I couldn't even think about sleeping. Was I dreaming? Was this really happening? Was the horse in the picture really Mirage?How could this be? Thousands of horses go through auctions every year and yet I was able to find him. My Mirage.

He would have to be quarantined. A friend offered to quarantine him in her barn. She had the perfect set up. Just a few miles from my farm. Now the wait.

Around 4pm I saw the truck and trailer. My heart is racing. This is really happening. When the horse stepped off the trailer I started crying. Yes, this was happening. It was my boy. Mirage. Hello my friend. I never forgot you. I never stopped looking.

NELLIE

Submitted by PAM

A picture of a 6 month old colt was posted by a friend on the facebook page Out Of The Kill Pen. It was a picture of the cutest Buckskin baby you would ever lay eyes on. The colt was in a Louisiana kill pen. It was reported the colt was an orphan Quarter Horse colt with good breeding. I shared the picture on my Facebook page and within a few minutes my friend, Cathi, sent me a text she was going to bail the colt and have him shipped to Maryland.

I was so excited for her. We were not only friends but we were practically neighbors. Our farms were only a few miles apart. I was going to get to enjoy her journey with her new res- cue colt. She paid the bail to the kill pen and found a lady to pick him up and transport him to Alabama for quarantine. The colt was picked up and transported to the quarantine farm in Alabama. Cathi received a few pictures of the colt on a stock trailer with the processing number glued to his rump.

Everyday I would call Cathi and inquire about the colt and when he was going to be making his way to Maryland. Days turned to weeks and the colt was still on the same stock trailer parked in a lot with no shade. As the pictures were being sent to update on his condition I could see he was losing weight.

Every time I asked Cathi why he was still in Alabama she would have another excuse as to his coggins test, his health certificate and trailering arrangements. The colt was literally starving to death before my eyes.

Four weeks and still no colt and he was running out of time. The quarantine facility housed the colt on the trailer for weeks with little or no food and water. The colt had gone from horrible conditions of a kill pen to a horrible quarantine farm. I pleaded with my husband, Mark, to help me save this beautiful colt. We already had 7 horses and our barn was full. We agreed to do what ever we could to help this colt. I contacted my best friend, Libby, and together we decided to make an intervention.

I contacted the lady in Alabama that was holding the colt and found out Cathi abandoned the colt and still owed money for board and quarantine. She no longer wanted the colt and didn't want to tell me the truth. I also found out the colt was a filly. A beautiful filly in dire need of a miracle. Libby and I decided to pay the outstanding debt at the quarantine farm and buy the filly. Her condition was deteriorating and we needed to get her transported to Maryland as soon as possible.

I contacted, Lexi, a lady in New York who hauls horses and she loaded her trailer, gassed up her truck and was heading towards Alabama by late that afternoon. The fee for hauling from Alabama to Maryland was going to cost a pretty penny but we were determined to give this filly a chance. Lexi arrived at the farm and loaded the precious cargo.

A picture was sent to me of the filly and a bay yearling loaded on Lexi's trailer. She had bought a yearling colt from the quarantine farm that was in need of a better life. Lexi has a huge heart and I had tears in my eyes knowing she was taking 2 young horses away from that horrible farm. Two days of hauling and Lexi pulled up at Libby's farm where the filly would be quarantined. I was at work when they arrived but my husband and Libby would be the welcoming committee. When the trailer door was opened there was a moment of silence.   The filly was laying down in a bed of straw and all you could see was a skeleton under her fur. My husband said he has never been so shocked by an animals condition as he was when he saw the filly. She was so weak she had to be helped off the trailer and into her stall. The vet came early the net morning and accessed her condition and she had a 1 body score. Her condition was critical and the next 7 days would be her turning point. Starting the filly back on a road to recovery had to be carefully planned and a refeeding schedule was written out by the vet. Libby started calling the filly Nellie and it suited her to a tee. " Nellie" it was. Nellie was so weak she could only stand for about 30 minutes at a time.

I would lay in the stall with her and keep her company in the pasture while she was grazing so she would never be alone. I wanted
her to feel loved and wanted. Her rehabilitation was a group effort and Libby, Mark and I rallied around Nellie every minute we could. The first week passed and we could see small improvements in her condition. She was gaining weight and we could see her personality shining through. After 30 days we moved Nellie to my farm and introduced her to another rescue horse in my barn, Mirage. They became instant friends and love each other.

Nellie has been in our family for 2 years now and she is

so smart and beautiful. Nellie and Mirage are finally in their forever homes and will always be loved. Nellie has added so much to our lives and we are truly blessed to be her family. She loves people and is the first to greet us when we walk through the pasture. She always sticks her nose to our face for a kiss on the nose. She is so cooperative with her training and always wants to please.

THE CROOKED COLT

Submitted by MARCY

I saw an ad online for a free colt that had a crooked leg. I had to go check him out, not that I needed a horse, but something about him drew me in. The ad stated that as he was growing, one leg went out to the side.

I got to the farm and saw a beautiful 2 month old colt with BOTH legs splayed out to the sides! The owner stated that they didn't even notice it growing strange because he was out in the pasture with his mom, where she had given birth and they had never checked on them until a few days ago. They wanted the colt gone asap so they could re-breed the mare.

I told them that I would take him, and loaded him into the back of my van! Yes, my vehicle! I was not leaving him there! I immediately took him to a teaching vet hospital near me, and asked what they could do for him!

I was told that IF he even made it, because of being so young and away from his mother, it would be a long process of trying to straighten his legs. They actually agreed to do everything for free as a learning experience for students!

Fast forward 2 months and the cold it growing stronger, and has his front 2 legs in soft casts. He is acting like a normal foal and loves people! He is a school favorite! Things are looking up for him!

He stayed in the casts for the first full year and a half of his life!

So here it is 6 YEARS later, and the crooked colt is still crooked, but not as bad as when he was a baby- he can run and play with other horses, but is still a bit limited as to other things like running as fast as they can. He has the cutest way of doing things because of his handicap but he is with us forever, and will be doted on and loved until his last day!

HIGGINS

Submitted by MELISSA

I had a friend. 'L', who had a bad fall off her mare. She was so scared after that she sold her horse. I was there when it happened and it was not the horses fault. We had been trail riding when the mare lost her footing going up a steep hill, and fell over backwards, pinning my friend underneath her.

After about a year, I talked her into going riding on one of my older quiet horses. Just one short trail ride. I could tell she was nervous, but after she mounted, and we took off, a short ride turned into a few hours! She was back in love with riding again!

A few months after, I got a call from her to come see her new horse! I could not believe she had jumped back in and was thrilled! Of course I rushed over to her place to see the new one!

When I got there I saw the most beautiful paint standing in the stall. This horse was huge. Built like a tank, and almost 16 hands! 'L' had bought him online and had him shipped in! He was a working cow horse, and had had the trip from hell, being on the trailer for about 32 hours because of issues with the shipper. He was so sweet and gentle though! BUT- I was concerned because my friend got him off the trailer and put him right into a stall, not letting him walk around and stretch his legs or roll.

I told my friend that he needed to exercise a bit before being stalled, but she knew it all and said he was fine. This bothered me, as I watched my friend with Higgins, I could see the uncertainty in the way she approached him to groom, she was really nervous! I started to ask her if she was sure this was the right horse, and pointed out that she seemed unsure of him, She assured me he was fin and so was she! I left later and still had a nagging feeling about the whole thing.

A few weeks later I get a call from her telling me there is something majorly wrong with him and she is going to sell him if she

can get him up. "GET HIM UP" What did she mean by that! I rushed right over there to see what she was talking about!

When I got there, this big beautiful horse she had only had a few weeks, was lying in the field, skinny, and moaning in pain! I asked her what happened, and she said he was too much to deal with and he had foundered and had abscessed on at least 3 feet! She wasn't going to keep him and would sell him to whoever wanted him!

I offered her $100 for him and she said get him gone! I went back with my trailer and it took an hour just to get him up and loaded. Once at my barn, I led him into a stall, and had the vet come immediately. My vet said he was not foundered, but did have abscesses and had his feet trimmed WAY too short!

I talked to my friend about this and she finally admitted that she was scared of him. There was no reason, she just wan not ready to have a horse again. She thought she was over her fear, but when she saw the size of this guy getting off the trailer, she knew then she wasn't ready! But she was embarrassed to admit it because she had bragged to everyone about how much this horse cost her, not including shipping! She didn't want anyone to think she was wimping out....

Well, as time wore on, Higgins got better and better. He was a gentle puppy type of horse! When we could finally ride him, we saw that he knew his job with cues and such for reining! We were all shocked! We knew he had worked cattle, but watching him slide to a stop and spin were amazing to us all! And on the trails, well, it takes a LOT to spook him! So much as a matter of fact, that in the 5 years of having him, we still haven't found out anything he spooks at! Even having shot a gun off of his back!

My friend still doesn't ride, and has no interest in horses anymore, which is probably better for her, because if she cant get over her fear, then she is likely to get injured again.

Higgins is our go to lesson, beginner, trail, show, and moving cattle horse here at the barn and we would not trade him for anything!

AXEL

Submitted by JORDAN

Horse #441, now known as Axel, is an 18hh crossbred gelding who went through the New Holland auction, and then the Cranbury Auction where I found him.

It's not for certain, but I believe it's fairly obvious that he was Amish born and raised. I had been looking for a horse with his exact specifications (height, age, gender, movement) for about 6 months, and actually decided to stop looking for a while when his picture and video came across my Facebook news feed... I couldn't pass him up!

Axel's amazing movement and gentle personality despite being so big were everything I was looking for in my next equine partner! Penny Parker proxy bid for me at the auction, and I didn't think I'd get him after the opening bid... but he was meant to be mine and Penny made it happen!

Unfortunately, he had to spend the next 97 days in quarantine for the Strangles virus. He was a little underweight, and used this time to put on some serious pounds! It helped that the staff fell in love with his sweet, puppy dog personality.

After the uncertainty of auction and a long stay in quarantine, he finally arrived to me in North Carolina 3.5 months later. I couldn't be happier with my big guy! He's very curious and brave as well as a quick learner and so willing to please! We're preparing for our first dressage show, and he is also showing great aptitude for jumping! He's the horse I was dreaming of, and I'm so happy and proud that I could pull him from the auction pipeline.

JEWEL

Submitted by HANNAH

J ewel was at End of the Line Horse Placement where she had caught my eye on their Facebook page but I just didn't have an option for quarantine at the time. Lucky for all of us she was bailed out by FOCUS Rescue and Rehabilitation.

She spent 30 days in quarantine and then ended up at my friends, 5 minutes away from my house. My friend Alisha told me what an absolute sweetheart she was and I knew we must go meet her. .

We had been keeping our eye out for a prospect for my 9 year old daughter. My 3 year old daughter and I went over to meet Jewel and it was a done deal at first sight.

Less than a 2 weeks out of quarantine and she was home. This lovely little mare took right to my 3 year old and showed AMAZING patients, tolerance and calmness. We took Jewel home just a couple days later.

She has been a complete blessing and a perfect fit my my oldest daughter, Makayla and a saint with my youngest, Jordyn. It is so hard to believe someone just threw her away because she is an absolute gem!

My 3 year old always leads her around after Makayla rides and no matter how hard my little one tries to get her to trot on the lead with her, she will just not do it. She just knows better! She will trot just fine with the older kids and adults but not my tiny tot..

I've actually seen her on several occasions intentionally offset her front hoof to avoid stepping on Jordyn (3 year old). Makayla has actually been a little reserved with riding different/new horses but with Jewel she rode her after only a week and showed her a week later! Jewel and her make a perfect team and Makayla is so excited to show this spring/summer and at fair this year! She is the perfect amount of
spirit and wisdom for both my girls!!! She's a beautiful pony and we are so proud and lucky to have her in our lives!

PRINCE

Submitted by CHRISTINA

Prince the Grade Arabian went through New Holland then wound up with another chance for horses.

The first video I saw of him he was cantering down a road and a plastic shopping bag blows down the road and hits him. When he didn't bat an eye I knew he was the one.

After bringing him home he got some groceries and proved to be the most bombproof in the barn under saddle. He got along with everyone and was mouthy and played like a 2 year old. He was my partner in crime for long trail rides, parades, local shows, and 4-H shows. We even did a clinic that Cris Cox selected him to do at equine affaire. We would go out cut down and drag a Christmas tree home every year.

One winter I remember coming home to him colicing. The vet came tubed him, administered banamine, and gave us specific instructions that we followed, as this was not the first time he had coliced. The next day he was even worse. With the option of surgery we weighed the options.

With the very low chance of survival and full recovery from surgery we made the hard decision to euthanize. He was the horse that taught us everything from beginning to end. We couldn't have asked for a better horse.

FANNIE

Submitted by JESSICA

My grandparents bred and raised Arabians when I was born, so I've been into horses my entire life. My grandpa passed when I was 4, and my grandma passed when I was 25. My grandma was the sole reason I was into horses and especially Arabians.

Even though she had to sell the majority of her stock when he died, she still stayed involved in the Arabian community. She took me to riding lessons and went to every show she could to support me. I showed an Arabian through most of my youth, but because the barn I was riding at, I ended up getting a quarter horse when I became an amateur. Although I still had a love for Arabians, I had no immediate intention of having another.

When I lost grandma on July 16, 2008, I lost the person

who shared my passion of horses with and felt so lost. I no longer had someone eager to hear how my ride went or if we nailed our canter leads that day.

Although I didn't know it at the time, on May 16, 2009, my life changed forever - I met Echos Fantasy aka Fannie. She was a thin, eight year old registered Arabian mare stuck at a low end auction barn. I fell in love with her the first time I saw her in her holding pen before the sale. There was just something about her that spoke to me. I can't fully explain it, but there was some-thing in her eyes and her kind face. It was that moment that I knew I needed to buy her. I'd always just had one horse and had absolutely no intentions of getting a second, but on that day, that very thing happened. My boyfriend at the time asked what I wanted him to bid up to on her. I told him I'd easily go $600 and he looked at me like I was crazy because Arabians never go that high at this sale. Arabians were basically a bad word in that area. People didn't think highly of them at all. When she came through the ring, they just lead her through but said she'd been shown

and had points on her. I took a gamble on her being broke and got her for a measly $275. The only others bidding on her were kill buyers. I was excited but also had the thoughts of "oh my god, what did I just do?? I so don't need another horse!"

We got her back to his house and discovered at least partially why she was at the sale. Someone had made her an awful halter puller. If you got her anywhere remotely close to something she thought you were going to tie her too, the whites of her eyes would show like she was terrified and she'd run backwards and flip over. She also did this same trick when saddling. When you were trying to tighten her girth, she'd fall down multiple times before you got the saddle actually on her and secured. From her actions, I think someone tied her up and then tightened her girth too tight and too fast.

A couple days later, I was still wrapping my head around my purchase that weekend. I was looking at my calendar and realized something odd and rather shocking. I met and bought Fannie exactly 10 months to the day after my grandma had passed away. How weird is that? After realizing the 10 month anniversary, I started looking for other signs wondering if grandma somehow sent me Fannie. I know it sounds rather silly and I must say, I never really thought about anything like this before. I'd even venture to say I previously didn't believe in anything like this. But as I dug and looked deeper, I can't help but think she really did send Fannie to me to get me back into Arabians (I still had the quarter horse when I got Fannie). Grandma's birthday was August 10th(8/10). Fannie was 8 years old when I got her and the 10 signified the 10 month anniversary of her death. Pretty weird coincidence. We also competed in our very first show together on July 16, 2013. It was the local county fair show that grandma had come to watch me at many times. I realized the day after the show that it was the 5 year anniversary of grandma passing away. The show was on a Tuesday which makes it an even more of an odd coincidence.

I simply can't help but think that Fannie was somehow sent by grandma to be with me since she couldn't anymore. Fannie has a forever home with me, and has given me so much in our almost 10 years together. I've worked through her halter pulling and cinchy issues. She now saddles fine, ground ties, and is my go to horse if I have a beginner or child wanting to ride. She's so sweet, careful and always takes care of her rider. I 100% trust her.

When I first got Fannie, I just envisioned her to be my friend and trail horse. About six years later, I decided I wanted to try showing at some of the rated Arabian shows with her. I thought she could possibly do well at the Arabian Sport Horse shows, but it was new territory to both of us. I sought out the help of a local Arabian trainer to take lessons with. We were talking about her and how I got her. He got this look of shock on his face and told me that he knew this mare. He said he couldn't believe this was her because she used to be hot and just awful. She came to him halter pulling and falling down with the saddle. He never could fix her of that. He said she also used to flip over backwards if you pushed on her too hard under saddle. Luckily, she never tried that with me! I also found out that it was a girl that worked for him that actually put the hunter pleasure points on her that I saw when I looked up her show record with the Arabian Horse Association. He also told me how she ended up at the sale – something I'd wondered for years. Her previous owner did really care about her, but she was diagnosed with cancer and died soon after. Before her death, she gave Fannie to this couple that the wife claimed she just loved Fannie. It was the same people who dumped her at the sale barn being under weight. At least her owner tried to do right by Fannie.

So apparently, it was meant to be. Fannie lost her owner and I lost my grandma. We needed each other and became a great team. In 2016, we attended our first Arabian Sport Horse show and got a second in Sport Horse Under Saddle which qualified us for Regionals.

We went on that same year to win at the Illinois State Fair in the Arabian Hunter Pleasure Mares or Stallions class. It was my first win at the state fair! In 2018, we tried the sport horse division again. This time, we added intro to western dressage and won the class at the pre-show to Regionals. At the Regional show, we were only a half point off from bringing home the reserve regional championship in that class. The next day, to my utter surprise, we brought home a regional championship in Arabian Sport Horse Under Saddle Amateur Owner To Ride! It was the coolest thing to accomplish on her with our past and unique story! It meant so much because her rehab and training was done by me! Yes, I had lessons from trainers here and there, but honestly, it was her and I trusting each other that accomplished this. She will forever have a home with me.

I guess the moral of the story is that things happen for a reason and you never know when you might find that once in a life time horse. Take chances on the "problem horses" and the sad ones at the sale barns. You never know what their story is, and what your story could be together!

LEONIDAS AND EVITA

Submitted by AMY

W hen I was growing up, like many other children, I found that I had a love for animals. All kinds of animals, but boy oh boy, did I have a passion for horses! Just wow, right?! I had plastic model horses, my pretty pony dolls and stable, you name it! The beauty, the strength, the fluidity of movement, the agility... who wouldn't want the friendship, companionship, and returned love from a horse? Well by the time I was 9 years-old, I had a few pay-by-the-hour trail rides under my belt, and I was 100% HOOKED!

Some months later, we bought a trail horse for $500. She was skinny, her coat was dull, she was dark, she was a back-jarring Quarter Horse, her name was Carmella, and I thought she was the most beautiful thing I had ever seen. I loved her every day of her life and have mourned her every day since her passing.

By 13, I had my first job shoveling out horse stalls at the

barn and I just knew that THAT was where I wanted to be. I would need to do something, ANYTHING, to be able to work with horses again at some point. This dream was not going to be easy as I was a kid from the inner city of Boston, Dorchester to be exact, not quite a place you'd want to vacation. Imagine more like the place where stolen cars were stripped then lit on fire on the back street behind our "triple-decker" (BONUS: Knowing what a triple-decker is). If you're familiar with the movie "Black Mass" about the infamous mob boss James "Whitey" Bulger, then you know of the concrete-ghetto neighborhoods where I grew up.... but I digress.

As the years went on, my dreams of horses and owning a stable were inevitably put on the back burner, typically where most childhood dreams end up, while one gets busy with a "real job" in the monotonous world of adulting. However, did I mention I left this particular dream on simmer???

There's not many things as tenacious as the dreams of a child, especially this child, because today, I am the proud and very happy owner of my own stable that currently houses 4 horses. Two of the
horses, I am somewhat torn to admit, I purchased. I have always

been a huge advocate of adopting animals and for me to purchase animals is a rare occasion. The good news is that the other 2 horses were rescued from a feedlot/kill pen, where horses sit until their number is picked for them to ship to be slaughtered. The bad news is the average person looking to purchase a horse has NO IDEA that there is such an immense and immediate need for horse rescue.

Only through purchasing horses and subsequently networking through horse groups on social media was I made aware that thousands and thousands of horses were meeting their untimely deaths and the hands of Kill Buyers. I had spent years working with Boxer dog rescue organizations and never once was I aware that horses shared the same plight of being thrown away in record numbers with the repeating cause to be the irresponsibility and greed of humans.

What kind of horses end up waiting in line for slaughter and are in need of rescue, was the very first thing that crossed my mind. After some quick and easy research, I could not believe what I was finding. Many were healthy and sound! Some young, old, green-broke, broke-broke, broke-to-ride, broke-to-drive, ponies, mini-horses, draft horses, mules, kid's horses, beginner safe horses, trail horses, gaited horses, registered horses, school masters..... you get the point. All of them, for whatever reason, were abandoned, and all of them deserve better. That's where rescue comes in!

Why I rescue is probably a novel in itself. It's one of those things that is equally rewarding and heartbreaking, and I'm sure every rescuer at some point has asked themselves (through tears and gritted teeth), "What in the *&@% am I doing this for??!?!" This story, however, is about who was rescued and I am really excited to share! Leonidas, an 11-year old grade (not registered) Paso Fino gelding, was dumped at a feedlot in North Carolina. He was stripped of his name and given a number (he was 601) that was stuck onto his skin, no different from how a package of meat at the supermarket is labeled. I suspect that some of the individuals providing horses for slaughter would frown on past owners being notified by new owners,

perhaps revealing the truth to them that their beloved horse who they thought they sold to a "forever home" was posted on a "last-chance-to-save-me" social media page before they were sent for their last ride. Was this the scenario that played out for Leonidas? Was his owner tricked into letting him go with someone who had planned ahead to deceive and sent him to his demise? I will really never know.

Leonidas was a good weight, handsome, he looked well taken care of, he appeared healthy, and he appeared sound. He had shoes on, all 4, and was said to have "been ridden for many miles on the trails". Leonidas had a video of him being ridden at the feedlot that was posted with his ad listing him for sale. In his riding video, he was amazing. He had a lovely gait, he moved out when asked, he cantered, he stopped, he appeared responsive to the rider; he was very alert with ears forward and eyes bright. The video almost prevented me from bailing him out and bringing him home. Leonidas was clearly too good to be true! There had to be something wrong with him. I read his ad easily a thousand times and watched his video at least two thousand, searching for some between-the-lines hidden meaning or examining his movement for any little hiccup. There was nothing discernible, and even if there was, I had watched his video so many times at one point, that I pretty much felt I had already bought him! That was it; reason be darned: I was getting him.

It was August of 2018, I already had 2 horses, and was about to get a 3rd, when all of a sudden it happened again. While making arrangements to bailout Leonidas, I am of course continuing to monitor the feedlot page. Coincidently, a group of 6 Paso Fino horses had arrived at the feedlot around the same time as Leonidas, all from the same farm. Now this group was definitely a group I would expect to see waiting for their doom at a kill pen. These horses were emaciated, ill, they were tied in a row in their video as the commentator talked about each one briefly, presenting either partial or full registration papers for each one. They were deflated, sad, and

stared blankly ahead with large lifeless eyes. Clearly, they had spent a significant amount of time being passed around and were
slowly starving to death. In spite of all this, I see that one by one, they are beginning to be marked as "safe" meaning someone has stepped up for the animal, paying the appropriate fees and committing to purchase the horse to give them another

chance. Their ship date is looming closer but they are all going to homes. All except one. A small, sick, grey little 10-year-old Paso Fino mare is still hanging around the feedlot on the afternoon before her scheduled ship date and all her friends have been adopted. That was it; reason be darned: I was getting her.

After a month of quarantine in North Carolina for my rescues (standard procedure), I decided I was going to pick up my new friends and drive them home to Florida! This was my first horse rescue, and somehow I managed to turn it into a 2-horse rescue, but luckily, I am married to an excellent partner who shares a passion with me for animals (thank goodness, right?!). In addition to this, it so happened that a friend of mine was also rescuing a Paso Fino horse from the same group of 6, so I offered to also pick up his horse for transport to him in Florida. Now I have a 3-horse rescue operation happening!

I'm happy to report we all made it home in one piece, and I am thrilled to report that there is nothing wrong with Leonidas, and that is why I wanted to share his story. I would like for people to know that the horses who find themselves at a feedlot or kill pen are worthy of a second chance, and they are not all lame, sick, dangerous, or unable to be trained. Leonidas came to me with some unavoidable emotional issues from his time being abandoned and trying to find his way on his own. He was nearly impossible to get into the barn from the paddock because he had been repeatedly lassoed and mistreated in quarantine. He would paw nonstop and was very anxious. He understandably lost some trust for people, but I could see that he didn't lose it completely. It was apparent from the way he watched me, leaning in to investigate and nuzzle me on the back when I wasn't

looking directly at him that he didn't lose hope for finding a family to bond with him.

Leonidas only needed some patience and time to know that he will always be taken care of and he will never be left behind again.

Today, he stands at liberty, untied, and the pawing is almost non-existent. He also lounges at liberty, stops and comes to me when asked, and he will also come into the barn with me at night without the use of a lead rope.

My other rescue, renamed Evita, is also doing fantastic. She certainly had suffered greatly but in spite of everything, Eve has allowed herself to participate in life again. It warms the heart to see them thriving and happy, and for all the tears and worry, the happiness they bring me makes every minute of it all worth while.

Thank you for allowing me the opportunity to share our stories!

THE BELGIAN

Submitted by KATELINN

My name is Katelinn. I've got a real rescue story. Its kind of long but quite the adventure.

It happened February 2007. I was 14 at the time. I was working at a dealer/ rescue. They would occasionally make the trip down to New Holland to pick up horses. That particular day they were supposed to auction off 200 minis. It was my first trip down, my mom gave me some money for the trip and I joked that I might buy a mini. She didn't tell me no.

The farm owner was a crippled old man with polio in a wheel chair, An old school shyster. several other girls and I were to go with him to handle the horses and help him get around. In retrospect, sending several 14 year olds with an old man to a horse auction probably wasn't the smartest idea. We left Sunday so we could be there early to get a look at the horses. Minis galore, ponies, drafts, you name it same old new Holland. He sent us girls to walk the barn and see what there was that night when we arrived.

Back in a corner was a Belgian, some kind of percheron cross and a standardbred. The standardbred and Belgian were in poor shape. We passed them over and found a few we were interested in. The next day the auction started. The old man had me help him choose a few horses, and taught me the art of bidding. This lady walks up and starts asking us if we could take one of the horses she brought with her. She heard we were a rescue and was claiming that he was to skinny to go through the ring and she absolutely can't bring him home.

Apparently she was a supposed rescue and was charged with neglect by the ASPCA because she was trying to keep 50 horses on 5

acres. She was told to re-home them immediately or face charges. I don't know if she had run out of options or what for her to decided to

unload horses at New Holland, I guess I'll never know why she brought them there. The old man refused, he wasn't interested in them. I couldn't get it out of my head. The lady came back a second

time he still refused. I wandered into the back and found him. He was standing tied to the wall all alone, the other horses she had brought already had been sold off at that point.

I walked up to him, he looked so depressed. His hair was super thick, hiding how skinny her really was. I went to his head and looked in his eyes. He just pressed his big head, half the size of me in my chest, my heart melted. I couldn't leave him there.

I went to the old man and tried to convince him to take him. He still refused. He told me to offer the lady $50 and see if she would take it. I tracked her down and made the offer. She refused, so defeated I went back and continued to watch the auction. A little while later the lady came up to me and said ok, we went to the office and I made it a legal sale. Here I am, 14 and just bought myself a starved Belgian for $50. Before it really had a chance to set in this Amish guy comes up to me yelling, claiming he was going to buy that horse for $250. He was livid, and kept trying to force $50 on me to take the horse. I kept refusing, but he made me take the money. At this point I had the horse vet checked and ok'd to make the long haul back to CNY.

This Amish guy just wouldn't let up, he started saying, and I Quote. "I was going to take that horse out back and stick a needle in his neck." Almost as if he didn't know that I knew what that meant. He was trying to take advantage of the fact that I was a young girl. I managed to loose the guy and went back to the old man and told him what happened. He went and reported this to the vet who he was good friends with. Turns out the Amish guy was one of the ring stewards and was not supposed to do stuff like that. So he got chewed out by his superior and came to me and apologized. I gave him back his $50.

Drama done, auction over, horses loaded in the trailer. It finally sunk in that I just bought that horse, not the old man. I was terrified of

what my mom would say and couldn't bring myself to call her. The old man did, she was proud and said she would have done the same thing. I left saying I'd buy a mini and came home with a Belgian.

He was a really rough shape and in his late teens/ early 20s. We kept him for a few months before we found him a home. They kept him for a few months before returning him and a pony we had gotten at the same auction at no fault of either of them. They had fattened him up really good and later that year he went to a new home to be a husband type trail horse!

Carrie Emerson-Boyd

SNOWY ROSE

Submitted by KIM

I t was a warm September day 1995. I had been taking riding lessons at a local barn for the past year, and I had saved every penny that I could find for my entire life. I had saved up $600 and decided it was time to get my first pony.

My best friend had also been riding at the local barn, and her parents
were taking her to the local horse auction to buy her first horse. I decided that I should ride along. All of my requests at my home to get a horse, or go to the auction were denied, but that didn't matter to me.

The horse auction was held once a month at the local livestock sale barn. It has small animal enclosures with a cat walk up above. As I walked the cat walk a light gray pony mare caught my eye. I had to get a closer look. I made my way down to the enclosure and met eyes with a beautiful solid gray appaloosa pony mare. She was solidly built with a large blaze, white stockings, a large white spot on her side, and mottled skin around her eyes and mouth. It was truly love at first sight. I located the owner, a horse dealer, and requested to ride the mare. He agreed but did not offer up any tack. So I rode this beautiful creature bare back with a halter and lead ropes through the aisles of the auction barn. She was perfectly behaved on the straight aisles, but would rear into the air at the corners. I did not care a bit about this behavior, I was in love.

I pleaded and through my persistence convinced my family to agree to contribute some money for this pony that stole my heart. I was certain she would bring more money than what I had been able to save. My friend's family graciously offered to let me keep any horse
that I purchased at their place with a horse that they would be buying for my friend. They had found a sad, emaciated thoroughbred mare
hidden in one of the back enclosures to keep her condition from being broadcast. My friend's dad thought this would make a fine first horse for my friend, and that in her condition he could get the horse for a good deal. He offered the owner $500, which was gladly accepted before the sale.

I waited anxiously for the gray pony to come into the sale ring. My friend's dad agreed to bid for me. She entered the ring decked out in western gear with a wanna be cowboy on her back. The ring is a small circular area designed to showcase cattle and sheep. The pony was not cooperating with the rider one bit. The only thing she would do is rear straight up. I was not worried one little bit about her behavior in the sales ring, I was certain it was just a normal reaction to a scary environment.

My friend's dad proceeded to bid on my behalf. The price continued to rise, my heart was in my chest. The bid price went above the money that I had available. Everyone in the stands was looking at us. The tension was palpable. I did not have the final bid. The auctioneer was practically begging me to
bid again. My friend's dad was looking at me for instructions on

what to do.   There were tears in my eyes at the thought that this beautiful pony might not be mine today. He offered to loan me the difference so I could get that one last bid in. I obviously agreed, and everyone practically cheered. I had won the bid on the pony that won my heart. Tears streamed down my face, I was in shock.

I knew immediately that I would name her Snowy Rose. My pony and my friend's horse were transported to her house the following morning. We spent
hours grooming them, leading them, riding them. I did not have a saddle yet, and my girl was frisky. I tried riding bare back, she would rush towards the paddock fence, stop short and spin hurling me into the dirt. I would brush off, catch her, push her up to the fence and jump on again. We repeated this
ridiculous scene all day. My friend's thoroughbred was quite skinny,

and thus very quiet for us kids to ride. We took turns walking around on her bareback with a halter and lead.

High School came, and with it came a new friend for me. She lived on a nice horse farm near the school. Her place had a proper

riding ring, barn with stalls, and many trails through the woods, and
along the river. Her mom was a riding instructor and they offered to bring my Snowy to their farm to help
me with her training. She was still quite a hand full. My old riding instructor had helped a lot, she found the proper bit for my girl so I could actually get her to stop before throwing me into the fence, but the rearing was still a problem.

After moving my pony we progressed quickly with the help of my new friends. She went from a snarky, naughty pony to a trusting sweet beginner lessson pony. She would gallop with me through the fields, snaking her head to grab a bite of corn. We would race the other kids with their Arabian ponies.

We spent nearly every day riding in the woods or swimming the horses in the river. I gave riding lessons to my nieces and to my friends sisters. But I caught the jumping bug, and my Snowy was no jumper.

So as it often happens, it was time to move on to a full size horse and find another home for my 14.1 hand gray pony. I worked on an ad, loaded with photographs of my sweet pony.

My Snowy was sold to a riding school for use in their summer camp program. I knew the stable owner and had faith that she would be well cared for, and get to teach a lot of new riders. I did not worry about the sale, everything seemed perfect.

I inquired with the stable owner late that same year, and she had sold my pony to another riding stable a little further from home. I checked with that stable owner, I was assured that they loved my Snowy and would give her the best of care.

I waited a full year and went to check up on my pony. She was not there. The farm had sold my pony to one of the lesson kids. The farm would not give me the name or contact information.

Snowy was not my pony any more, so there was nothing more I could do but pray that she was loved and cared for.

March 2014. I was driving home from work and started thinking

about my beautiful Snowy. She would have to be nearly 35 years old,

if she were still alive. I let myself reminisce for a few moments, and pondered the whereabouts of my precious girl. I decided that she would most likely be passed away, and without any leads from the past there would be no way to actually know.

I was home with my baby daughter, spending time scolling through facebook as I often did. As I mindlessly scrolled a sad gray pony tied to a stock trailer made me stop and stare. My

mouth dropped open. Here was my Snowy Rose. But could that really be her tied to that kill buyer's trailer? Could that
actually be her with a threat of shipping to slaughter? They had her listed as an 18 year old, 14.1 hand mare. I pulled out old photos of my girl and compared markings. I was in complete denial. I contacted all my friends who had known my Snowy.

The first friend responded with no way. She would be ancient,
she was certain that Snowy would be deceased by now. I sent the pictures to another old friend who had known my girl. She compared the markings and said that it had to be her, and that appaloosa ponies live a very long time. I just knew that this was my pony. In the picture ad by the rescue I could clearly see that this pony had the big white marking on her side, the big white blaze on her face, and the stockings. This was no mere coincidence.

I now had to figure out how to buy back my beloved pony and get her home from four hours away. I went on the Facebook page and started spreading the word that this was my long lost pony. I began fund raising and pleading with strangers. A very sweet lady donated $150 in the memory of her
daughter's horse who had recently passed away. Another kind lady offered to pick her up off the kill buyer's feedlot and keep her at her farm until I could get her picked up. Unfortunately for me we were having large amounts of snow, I do not have a truck or trailer, and
shipping is very expensive. I got Snowy paid for, and moved on to the farm of a complete stranger.

I begged everyone I knew with a truck or trailer. Finally, a friend's
mom who had known my Snowy agreed to make the journey for the cost of fuel. We watched the weather forecast and decided to head out early one morning. We took a blanket to put on Snowy for the trip and started our way from Maryland into

Pennsylvania. After driving for over two hours my friend told me that the trailer brakes were not working. We were not stressing too much because the van brakes were working. We continued our trek. It was raining and sleeting while we drove. The rain was freezing on the roads making the trip scary, especially with no working trailer brakes.

According to our GPS we were less than ten minutes from the farm holding my dear pony. My friend anxiously stated that the brakes were not working on the van. She would push the pedal down with little result. There was not much we could do, we were so close to getting my pony.

We pulled up to the farm. A nice lady and her kids came out to meet us. They lead Snowy from the barn. I did not recognize my girl at first. She was skinny. I had never seen my girl skinny, she stayed fat on air. My friend asked worriedly if I was sure that was Snowy. I remembered the pictures and the matching markings, before we got here I was certain this was my Snowy.

We blanketed and loaded this poor skinny old pony onto my friend's little two horse trailer. We drove just down the street to a Walmart store parking lot. She managed to get the rig stopped with the emergency brake and we called her son. He walked us through a number of checks to try to find what was wrong with the van breaks and how to fix it. We determined that the brake line was leaking. We tried putting brake fluid in and clamping the hose unsuccessfully.

We were going to be waiting the four hours for her son to come rescue us in the Walmart parking lot. It was dinner time, I did not plan on an additional four hours of wait time. Luckily my friend had a bucket in her trailer. We went into the Walmart to get supplies and

dinner. I looked in the pet section and picked up a bag of chopped timothy hay intended for rabbits, in the hunting section I grabbed a bag of dried whole corn cobs intended for squirrel feeders. We grabbed a couple gallons of water and ordered some pizza. I spent about an hour in the freezing trailer with my pony. I think she remembered me. She kept placing her head on my shoulder and huffing. She was incredibly calm while I stood at her side.

My friend's son arrived with a large box truck to pull the trailer home. We drove that and her son took the van with no brakes. We limped home. We were slated to arrive at my farm just at nightfall, but with the additional 4 hour wait time it was well after midnight. I kept Snowy in a stall overnight at another part of the farm until morning. The truck and trailer would not have been able to turn around at my rented space on the large farm.

In the morning I went out and this time there was no doubt that I had brought home my Snowy Rose. She was much older, and much thinner, and she had small growths around her eyes causing her
eyes to water and secrete a yellow drainage. I rode her on top of the winter blanket from the front farm to my field. She was wonderful. This would end up being the only time I would ride my sweet pony.

I had the vet out to check her eyes within the week. The prognosis was not good. She had cancerous growths on both eyelids. We decided to try a chemo eye ointment to see if the growths would stop or recede. There was too much eyelid involvement to just remove the growths. Chemo was our
best option.

Snowy HATED the eye ointment. She would run from me in the field when she saw me coming with the ointment. It is no fun chasing a pony around a field in the snow and mud. One cold morning I took a friend, a new potential boyfriend, with me to help administer her dose of eye ointment. She ran from me and crossed the creek. I jumped the creek in pursuit, my boot got caught up in the mud and stayed, while my body continued it's forward projectory. I landed on my stomach in

the cold mud. My sock was completely soaked with brown half frozen mud. My new beau crossed the creek, retrieved my rubber boot, and helped me to my feet. I continued after Snowy, got her halter on her, and administered the eye ointment. This was a first date of sorts with this new boyfriend. He and I graduated high school
together. We reconnected just this same March after nearly 16 years.

Snowy quickly picked up weight at my farm. She became fast friends with my other horses.

My daughter had a couple of pony rides on Snowy. Unfortunately, her eye melanoma was progressing and the chemo eye ointment was not making a difference. The vet offered only one other solution, to remove her eyes and eyelids. I did not feel that this was the right decision for a 35 year old pony, even though she was perfectly healthy in every other way. When the cancerous growths started to impact

Snowy's happiness, they were rapidly enlarging, we decided it was time for euthanasia. I made the arrangements and met the vet with Snowy for the last time in November 2016. I got to be there with my special pony for the end of her life. I petted her neck as the vet gave her the medications to stop her heart. Thankfully she left this world peacefully and with a full belly. I cried for days. I had lost my mom to cancer nearly ten years prior on the same date.

Despite the ending I feel incredibly lucky to have my pony back for her last years. I know that
she had a good retirement and end of life. I know that she left this world surrounded by the love of a little girl for her pony.

FROM PLOW TO WOW!- APOLLO

Submitted By JACKLYN

(as reported in local paper)

NORTH BROOKFIELD -- If she wasn't spending every extra penny on her horse, Jacklyn Gearin might have a new car; maybe a snazzy fire-engine-red convertible to match her trademark slick lipstick.

"But I wouldn't be happy," she said sitting on an over-turned bucket outside the barn at Little Pond Farm, a friendly white barn cat clamoring for her attention.

"You have to have things in your life that make you happy, not powerful," she said.

Across the way a huge horse, Apollo, glistened in the sun. His sleek black coat caught the light as he turned to the sound of Ms. Gearin's voice, stomping his foot -- the signal that he wouldn't mind if she gave him a peppermint or an apple.

"We have a bond," she said of the 1-ton Percheron that was once half of a team of Amish plow horses. "We have a trust that doesn't come overnight. It comes after a lot of miles."

Apollo, 13 years old, is not the sort of horse one would normally throw a saddle on, though plenty of folks have ridden horses of the large breed. Ms. Gearin, who lives in Worcester and boards her horse in North Brookfield, said she'd never thought about it. But that changed when she was at The Big E in West Springfield watching the fair's horse show a couple of years ago and she saw riders in a category called "draft horse under saddle." The giant horses with riders aboard took her breath away, and she said to her ex-husband, "I'm gonna be in that show."

She remembers that he chuckled. Lenny Woodis had taught his former wife to drive Apollo and Zeus, the two big Percherons he got at auction 11 years ago.

"I had very little experience with draft horses," she said. "Except that when I was a kid growing up in Spencer our neighbor had one

and we would walk down there with my mother and call him and he'd come to see us. I called him Big Foot."

After some practice, she was able to drive the team around New Braintree when she lived there. She'd head to a local store, park the team and grab a hot chocolate before driving them back home.

She'd ridden horses as a child but developed asthma and allergies and quit when she was 9 years old. A few years ago, in her mid-40s she was ready to ride again, this time on Apollo, whose plowing partner, Zeus, has also taken to being ridden. "I got a $15 bridle at an auction in Pennsylvania and a saddle for $25 that I didn't exactly fit in," she said.

With makeshift reins, she took her first ride, and her dream was within reach. There was no indoor riding ring, so she simply plowed a track in one of the high fields and rode Apollo there. In almost no time, the pair clicked, the big horse reacting to Ms. Gearin's directions as though he'd been made for trail rides and horse shows.

She started taking the horse to smaller shows, for practice, and she noticed that when she walked Apollo off the trailer, heads turned and folks grew quiet.

"It was pretty cool," she said. "I liked it. What I really like is sharing Apollo with people. He's a very special horse."

Apollo became known for his gentle demeanor. This summer, 10-year-old Sophie Law of Brookfield, whose mother, Amy Law, is also a skilled rider, showed Apollo several times and did quite well.

Mrs. Law and Sophie are part of what Ms. Gearin calls "the A-Team," a group of Apollo fans who help at the barn, lend a hand at shows and cheer for their favorite horse and rider wearing "A-Team" shirts. Ms. Gearin often credits them on her Facebook page. On Friday, she'll take to the ring at the Big E, hoping to win her class. She'll arrive a few days early and will ride Apollo, wearing some

expensive, fancy gear, in the Coliseum during down time The show will be her second and she's already talking about next year when, after the Big E ends, the World Percheron Congress will come to the fairgrounds. "Oh, I'll be there for that," she said. "Just imagine it. And Sophie's going to ride in that, too. She'll be ready by then."

Ms. Gearin said she's worked in some high-stress jobs but has always been able to put that behind her when she climbs on her horse and the two of them gallop off through autumn leaves, snowy forests or spring buds.

"When I was a kid, I remember I'd ride the carousel and I would always pick the black horse with the most bling," she said. "Now I have that horse, and I just keep going around and around and it just gets better and better."

*(story as told to a reporter for a news paper)

THE NO NAME HORSE

Submitted by AMANDA

On March 13th 2017 I was scrolling through my Facebook when I came across a sad, emaciated horse on my homepage. She was in a kill pen in Arkansas and desperately needing a home.

They had posted a couple photos and video of this poor mare tacked up and being ridden, stood on, jumped on, and crawled under, I thought she seems so gentle especially for not knowing these people. She tugged at my heart strings for sure watching that video.

Knowing that we didn't need a third horse, especially not one so underweight and about six hours away, I went ahead and ran it past my then fiance. He needed a horse to ride anyways since my foxtrotter rescue couldn't be ridden and my other rescued gelding was a bit too much horse for him so it didn't hurt to ask right?

I was shocked when he gave me the go ahead! We drove from Missouri to Arkansas two days later to pick up this sweet girl. She seemed so much thinner in person, with saddle sores on her back, a big knee, and a leg injury actively bleeding when we picked her up.

She loaded with little hesitation and off we went back home to a new beginning for this poor, starved, unloved mare. When we unloaded her at home, she seemed so weak, she was given fresh water and hay and a blanket to keep her old bones warm in the cold Missouri March we were in. You could see almost every rib through a full winter coat on this horse, we weren't sure she'd make it through the night.

The next day we started her on a senior grain and found out the leg injury was worse than expected. The vets came out and tended to her injury, gave her an overall exam. Her leg looked awful and had suffered from a previous injury before the current one. They cut proud flesh off the leg without sedation, she was too thin to sedate, and was given antibiotics, we were told her front knee was arthritic, and she desperately needed her teeth done, they had major overgrowth and sharp points.

After about four months of proper feed, care and love my beautiful girl started to look like a horse again. We went for our first

ride since she put on enough weight, she was perfect. I have taken
her on a few short trail rides and two cattle drives. She has even given a child their first ride ever on a horse. She is a companion now to my other horses as we are dealing with some health issues with her as she ages.

She was thrown away like garbage, never even having

a real name, just a number, and worked hard by her previous "owners." She is the sweetest, gentlest horse who is worth her weight in gold.

I took a chance on a sad, starved, neglected horse and have received so much in return from her. She has a forever home with us now and we have promised her the best till its time to go, where we will be with her whenever that time comes. I love this little mare with all of my being and I am so glad I took a chance on what most people have considered "broken, a lost cause, and not worth the money." She is worth all of that and more.

CIMBER

Submitted by HANNAH

November 2013 I went out to an old boarding stables to look at a horse. I didn't have much info on him, besides they recently bought the horse and he was too wild for them and so they put him out in a pasture.

When I got there, there was this scrawny, depressed horse who had no joy or life in his eyes. I don't know what all was his past but I knew I needed to bring him home.

The owners were terrified of him but all I saw was a scared, depressed colt who needed TLC.

Within a week I had him broke. Within 2 weeks he started to show some personality and trust, And in 1 month we competed in our first Cowboy Extreme Challenge which is like an obstacle course on your horse that's times and judged.

Out of 30+ contestants, we brought home 7th place and a

check. After that it's just be one amazing thing out of that horse after another. He's taught me so much and I've taught him so much.

From day one to now he's gained over 350lbs, he was 4 when I brought him home and now he's 9. He's won over 10 belt buckles, 100s of dollars in tack, 300+ ribbons, 3 checks, and has won so many hearts on our journey.

He does roping, barrel racing, sorting, pole bending, Cowboy Extreme Challenges, Mounted Sheriff Patrol, and rescue unit. I couldn't imagine my life without this horse in it. He found his forever home that day.

THE TALE OF MY SHADOW

Submitted By HANNAH

Shadow was rescued in 2009. My dad used to listen to a radio hot-line every day. For two weeks Shadow was offered for sale, my dad felt moved to go see the horse.

Shadow was extremely underweight, in a very dangerous pasture, and had huge knots in his hair.

My dad offered half of the money, and if he lived a month he would pay them the other half to which they agreed. It took us 6 hours to catch him and load him onto the trailer, he was scared and showed signs of being abused. After years of hard work, Shadow trusted me. We did many shows, parades, and trail rides together.

THE TALE OF FLICKA

Flicka was rescued from new Holland sales stables back in April of 2018. Flicka was severely underweight. With love and attention she is now a little boy's first pony and the love of his life.

FAITH AND FRIENDS RESCUE

COPPER

Copper came to Faith N Friends around 6 years ago. Copper is a grade foundation quarter horse gelding (we do not have his papers). Copper was estimated to be around 8 years old when he came to us.

He has major trust issues for unfortunate reasons. Copper was bought by a young man at a sale when he was a yearling. That same man trained Copper but he never wanted to geld him.

The man came upon hard times and needed to get rid of Copper.

Copper was an 8 year old, very proud stallion, but Faith N Friends does not take in stallions and will geld all studs that come to us. The young man and his cowboy boss decided to geld Copper themselves after we had purchased Copper but before we picked him up.

Faith N Friends spoke with the young man and strongly disagreed with this idea of cowboy neutering! We ensured him we would have a veterinarian out to do this surgery. Unfortunately the young man and his boss became intoxicated one night and decided to geld him anyway. Copper was hogged tied, minimally drugged, and castrated. Supposedly it took 5 men to hold him down with hog ties around his legs.

The pain and stress Copper endured was unimaginable. When Faith N Friends came to get Copper his legs were swollen all the way down to his back hooves. You could not see where his knees began and his ankles ended. He had lost a tremendous amount of weight, had no life left in him, and did not want to move. Faith N Friends had a University of Tennessee Vet assess Copper and it was decided that the damage to his lymphatic system and tissue in his legs was too severe and that he would never be sound again.

Thankfully after 2 years of therapy, rest, and rehabilitation, Copper has made a FULL recovery! He is one of our best riding horses and shows no sign of lameness or swelling in his legs. However, Copper is very afraid of men in general and is harder to catch due to his unfortunate events. Due to Coppers issues he is not adoptable but has a forever home with Faith N Friends.

GRETTA

Gretta is a registered, well bred quarter horse, grulla mare whom we acquired from a different rescue in Tennessee in 2012.

Gretta was born in West Tennessee in May 2010. Her father was a very well bred Jac Cody, 86, red dun and her mother was a registered running bred AQHA bay. They produced a beautiful foal!

However, the elderly owner died shortly after she was born. Gretta along with about 30 other horses were left to fend for themselves until the family could figure out what to do with all the horses. Unfortunately by the time the family had got involved, Gretta had already endured a horrible injury.

According to the previous owner's son, Gretta got spooked from a backhoe and ran away from the herd and they did not find her until the next day.   She had jumped the chicken wire fence and got her back left leg caught up in it.

The son said she did not have any scratches or tears on her leg however when they got Gretta undone from the fence she refused to walk and only pivoted in a circle.

He said he gave her a week or so to try to recover but he did not call the vet; she was losing weight fast, her back left hip had atrophied, and she was barely walking. After about a week and a half he decided to put Gretta down. His girlfriend finally talked him out of it and said she would find a rescue for Gretta to go to.

Therefore, Gretta along with her half sister were donated to a West TN rescue, River Edge Rescue. The rescue had the vet come out immediately to assess Gretta. They X-rayed her legs and kept her in a stall for recovery. X-rays came back clean, and Gretta started to recover slowly.

When Faith N Friends saw her on the rescue's website we knew Gretta was for us! Faith N Friends would have loved to take her half sister too however we only had one opening and decided to let Gretta fill it! Since coming to Faith N Friends Gretta has blossomed! She is the head mare in our pack, put on a significant amount of weight and walks, trots, and gallops around the pasture! She has gone through rehabilitation to help her hip gain muscle. Gretta's hip is still not perfectly symmetrical to the other side, but she is now sound! Due to Gretta's injuries she is not adoptable and has a forever home with Faith N Friends.

LUCKY

Lucky was a rescue from a University Research facility. She was dropped off at the university from her owner that did not want her when she was only two years old. She had a hiatal hernia that had to be repaired. The University fixed her hiatal hernia and then used her for practice for their vet students. Lucky was at this facility for 4 years.

When we first saw Lucky it was evident that her research guinea pig days were over! We asked if we could have her and the University

was trying to decrease their number of horses so they surrendered her to us!

We started Lucky's rehab by letting her be a horse with no one probing or prodding at her! Once she figured out that we were not going to stick her with needles or poke and prod, she came around quickly! She was sent to the trainer and after 30 days was as good as any other!

Lucky is very dear to us, she is used for riding for our intermediate riders. She is a sanctuary horse and will live out her days with Faith N Friends! Everyone here loves Lucky, she is beautiful and so much fun to ride. On the day our volunteers exercise the horses they always fight over who will get to ride Lucky!

SOCKS

Socks was Faith N Friends' very first rescue. He is a 9 year old grade AQHA gelding. His mother was a Sonny Dee Bar bred AQHA and his father was a Mighty bred AQHA, however he was never registered and both of his parents are deceased.

Faith N Friends has had Socks since he was around 6-8 months old. Socks was an owner surrender from West TN. He came to us in good condition and enjoyed human company. Socks is very personable and loving.

He had a freak accident at the age of 3 that decreased his vision

in one of his eyes. After multiple vet visits and medicine we were able

to save his eye but he had lost some vision. Socks went to two different trainers after his eye injury had healed to be trained to ride. Both trainers sent him back saying he couldn't be trained due to his loss of sight in his eye. We knew socks would be a great riding horse so we decided to train him ourselves.

After 30 very long days and frustrating moments Socks was 'trained'. Socks was as good as they got, no buck, gentle, and reliable. He was used as a trail and lesson horse for the next 3 years.

From that point we noticed he started getting jumpy and spooky when we handled and rode him. We had the vet check him and found that he had lost all sight in the one damaged eye. We took Socks on his last trail ride at East Fork Riding Park in 2011. He did great, however he did spook a lot and we realized he needed to be retired.

Therefore, since then Socks has been a happy pasture pet and enjoys getting human company whenever he can! We decided to take Socks out of retirement and work with him again as he always loved to work and ride. Socks surprisingly did very well and every now and then enjoys going for short rides with a trusted rider. He is fat and happy and spends most of his time out in the pasture.

FAT CAT BERTIE

Fat Cat Bertie is the product of both the TB Industry and the slaughter industry! She is a 13 year old raced and tattooed thoroughbred.

When she came to us she had a body score of 1 out of 10. We quickly started her on a re-feeding program at her foster home! Her teeth were in very bad shape with a lot of sharp points, and she had abscesses too. But unfortunately, you really can't get any closer to death than she was and we really we not sure that she was going to even make it.

She is now doing wonderfully in her rehab program with her foster home Freedom Farms. They are taking their time and putting

the weight back on her slowly. We also want her to gain some muscle so once she has healed she can be assessed for riding.

Freedom Farms is run by patient, loving, and hard working people. They are out before the sun rises feeding and checking on Cat. They change her blankets or take them off completely depending on the weather and feed her three times a day. Cat really is feeling the love!

We have done some research and know a little bit more about her history. Cat was born on March 29, 2005 in Kentucky. Cat had 55 starts in her career, won 6 firsts, and earned over $58,000! Cat was bred four times in the last four years, but only foaled twice with a stud named Baptistry. She was bred just last April to a stud in Ohio named Much the Best however the breeding was not successful.

What we do not know is how Cat got from Ohio to an auction here in Tennessee. In March, Cat's previous owner purchased her from an auction in Mascot, Tennessee, not horribly underweight.

We were told that Cat picked up more weight but when another horse belonging to her previous owner had a foal and that horse and her foal were moved across the street, Cat stopped eating and would pace the fence. After she had dropped a significant amount of weight they finally decided to move Cat across the street as well. She was doing okay until board went up at the barn where Cat was at and they were forced to move.

Cat's new location was small with not enough pasture so her owner bravely decided to surrender her to us to be sure she would not end back up in the slaughter pipeline. Cat came to us without any record of vet, farrier, or dental work. We got a copy of her coggins taken at the auction.

Cat now eats three, two pound, $5 meals a day that consist of good feed and supplements, is on great grass 24/7, and is given hay as well. Cat is a perfect example of why we say a horse bailed from a kill buyer is not a horse rescued!

This horse has suffered, you can look at her and tell that in just a few months she went from being a healthy animal to being at death's door.

It's going to be a very long haul for Cat but we are dedicated to committing 100% to every horse that we take in. She deserves that, they all deserve that Cat is currently up for adoption however we will most likely not re-home her until she is completely rehabbed and healthy. After winter we will begin assessing her for riding and already have a volunteer trainer lined up to work with her.

ELFIE

Elfie is a 12 hand, approximately 15 year old pony. Elfie was the first recipient of our "Mercy Trimmings" program in which Faith N Friends helped her recover from severe founder and immensely long hooves in 2014.

Unfortunately, two years after Faith N Friends had gotten Elfie healthy her new owner had let her health deteriorate into a similar state again. Now Elfie is back with us, but this time as a live-in rescue, and we will be choosing her new home. As of intake she was in very bad shape – underweight, poor coat, upper respiratory infection, lice, and hooves at least 1.5 feet LONG! She is permanently crippled on her hind legs from foundering due to years of lack of care.

Upon settling in, Elfie's hooves were trimmed several times, she was given two lice treatments, was started on treatment for her respiratory infection, was started on a feeding schedule to gain weight, and had a sarcoid removed from her left eye.

Soon after intake Elfie's hooves were in good shape, her weight was good, coat was healthy, and she was able to walk better. A lot of TLC has been given to this little girl to get her back to par. Elfie will only be able to be a pasture companion and loving pet due to her crippled leg. She is great in herds and is currently a 12 hand giant in a field of mini horses and mini donkeys. Elfie will need a patient, gentle home as the neglect she has received at the hands of humans has made her weary of people. With patience she can be a loving girl who loves to be groomed.

Once Elfie was healthy enough, she went to the trainers, not for riding, but for ground manners, leading, handling, etc. We noticed Elfie's belly was getting bigger fast! Vets confirmed that she was going into her LAST trimester and was pregnant! Not exactly the surprise we were wanting... The vets doubted that she could be pregnant on intake due to her being severely malnourished and underweight, however she was housed with a mini stud whom we also rescued before coming into the rescue!

Elfie foaled her little baby Miracle and they were taken

by an adoptive family. Soon though, Elfie had to go to a foster home due to

having to wean Baby Miracle! Baby Miracle was sad at first but then learned about playing happily with her other herd mates! Elfie also did great with the move and enjoys her baby free life!

THE FINAL TEN

Submitted by Catelin

I t was a dark and stormy night... no, it was not. It was a bright and hot day in the west Texas feed lot, and about 110 degrees, in the shade. The horses were all sweaty, heads hanging low, and literally on the way to their last trip into Mexico.

I got to the auction just in time to hear the meat buyers talking about a group of mustangs that had just been brought in- all unbranded. The mustangs are easy targets when they are unaccounted for. The meat men can get them cheap and sell them into slaughter and make a decent profit!

I saw these mustangs, and they all looked defeated. Heads down, sweaty and one mare had a colt by her side that was no more than a few weeks old. It broke my heart to see them in captivity like this! I knew I had to do something!

I called a friend who has a large- over 1000 acre ranch in Montana and spoke with him about this, as he is a mustang preserve owner and already has two bands on his ranch. He told me to bid whatever I had to to be able to get them and we would get them to his ranch!

I was elated! The bidding on the group began, and I could not believe it when no one bid over $1500 for the lot! I went to $2000 and ended the bidding!

The next day I went back to pick them up with a large stock trailer to make the long trip to their new home. When I got there, they were crowded into a tiny pen together and the foal was on the ground! The horses were barely moving, trying not to step on him! They had no shade or water and not a trace of hay!

I cautiously went into the pen to check the foal. He was severely dehydrated, and not able to stand I picked him up- he was so tiny he was easy to lift! He did not even struggle, and his mother stood by just watching- almost like she knew I was trying to help!

I loaded him into the cab of my truck, and we got the rest loaded into the trailer. My first stop was the vet! We gave him IV Fluids, and the veterinarian gave me a few bags to take with me, so I could change them on the trip!

Well, a few hours into the trip, the colt started to gain a little life! He was sitting up like a dog in the back seat and making little noises! He was going to make it- but I was scared to put him in the trailer. Yep... this was going to be a long trip!

I finally made it to my friends house and as I pulled up, he came out to greet me. As soon as I got out of th truck, he said "why do you smell like a stockyard?". He got his answer as I got the colt out of the back seat. Lets just say, you can't exactly stop and walk him like you can a dog. Man, my tuck is going to need a good cleaning- like a hose out with a fire hose!

We evaluated the horses who all made the trip just fine, and unloaded them into a holding pen. Even the colt. His mother was very glad to see him! After a few days, letting them settle in- it was time to release them! Wow, what a sight to behold!

We opened the corral gate and after a few minutes- they took off out of there! The mare with the colt stopped a little ways off on top of a hill, and just looked at us. Like she was saying thank you! So all in all we saved 8 mares, one stallion and a colt!

To this day the herd is running free and wild!

BRAVO

Submitted By JULIA

J uly of 2017, I kept stumbling upon Facebook pages of kill pens. And being an animal enthusiast, who doesn't look at these souls and want to save them? I couldn't stop looking at a Grey gelding. It was between him and a paint mare. However, being only eighteen and still under my parents' roof, I knew it either wasn't going to happen, or be impossible. It was impossible for me, but God does impossible things!

I started looking into every aspect of rescuing a horse; prices, shipping, quarantine, care, etc. It seemed doable! But I kept messaging and emailing and calling and no one was getting back to me, until it was the grey geldings' ship date.

My parents had accepted that I had to do this. They encouraged me but also were weary.. seeing as you just don't know what you're going to get. I nearly gave up because everyone around me was worried about how he moved.   Long story short, they finally answered my call, and I was able to bargain for him, since he already shipped. Other rescuers at a Texas lot pulled him off for me, and sent him back to Louisiana, where I would pay a shipper to haul him 14 hours to southwest FL.

It felt like ages until I knew he was on the way. I was scared and excited. Thankfully we have our own stable, so I was able to prepare a stall for him in our outside barn that wasn't used at the time. But he never was sick.

The grey gelding was nearly the last stop - there was maybe one other horse on the trailer besides him when he got here. The poor thing looked so tired.. until we put him in his stall haha. I had friends that had previously rescued horses there helping me, if it weren't for them I probably wouldn't have bought him.. but we also had boarders who were scared out of their minds. I can't blame them, they thought he was going to spread shipping fever or a respiratory infection - however, it was a bit extreme. And it stressed me.

But I would do it all over again if I could. The couple of weeks of going to take care of a horse that I rescued was one of the most amazing experiences, and that was only the beginning. The following fall I would start riding him, and keep going from there. He taught me
as I taught him. And I grew frustrated so many times, but he's made me realize and learn how to work with so many other beings.

A year+ later, Bravo (like NATO phonetic alphabet), which I named him, is giving riding lessons, goofing off, learning tricks, making friends, and letting me dress him up as a unicorn for birthday parties. He loves every bit of it.

One of my favorite parts is the differences between him and my horse of 5 years – Bravo knows that I rescued him.

I'm still learning things about him.. as of lately, we've realized that he is not entirely Quarter Horse, but MO Fox Trotter too! He likes to show me his gait when trotting his eleven year old student around the ring.

Now my plans for him are to keep doing what he's doing, become and therapeutic horse, or possibly be a mount for border patrol. Nothing makes my heart more happier than when people see him, and say "That's a beautiful horse", and they didn't know that at one point in his life, he was hanging on for dear life.

These rescue horses are amazing! They can do anything! It shows that the Lord really watches out for His creatures!

EVA

Submitted By MEGAN

I was 13 and had been taking lessons since I was 6. I begged and begged for a horse of my own but we lived in a neighborhood and didn't know much about owning ourselves.

My mom had a friend who had a cattle farm and would sell hay as well. I went with them to deliver hay to a man only to find all of his horses emaciated, covered in ticks and overgrown hooves. He did surprisingly know their names but that seemed to be all he knew.

Following that visit I told my mom about these horses and how the sweetest but the most skinny little horse came and snuggled on me while they were standing there talking.

One day we went to visit my mom's friend and when we pulled up I saw the mare standing in her field with two others! I was so happy to see she got out of the mud pit she was previously in. My mom insisted we go and see them and give them treats, which was weird because my mom wasn't THAT into horses. We walked down the driveway back to the pasture where the mare was, as I was petting her, staring at her overgrown mane and visible ribs my mom told me she was mine! I was over the moon and could not believe it. I started spending all the time I could with her. We learned her name was "Ethel", she was six years old and bred in Pennsylvania.

It makes you wonder how she ended up in Virginia. Once getting to know her we renamed her Eva, since she really didn't know her name. A few years after getting her my family moved and bought land for Eva to come to in our own backyard! Eva is the most kind hearted horse I've ever been around. She LOVES kids and has given many pony rides, she has been a lesson pony for a 6 year old and takes care of her riders always!

Eva today is semi-retired from riding and is enjoying her days eating and relaxing with her thoroughbred friend, Remi.

CHOSEN
BY A HORSE

Submitted By KRISTIN

R ecent studies have shown that the electromagnetic field around a horses heart is believed to be five times as large as those of a humans, which varies between eight and ten feet in radius and with such strength behind it, horses are capable of directly influence our own heart rate.

I believe that was what had happened to me. It was just a little over three years ago when I met my beloved Luz de Luna (Light of the Moon), I immediately felt her "coherent" heart rhythm (heart rate pattern) which studies have found to be a robust measure of well-being and consistent with emotional states of calm and joy. That would explain the unexplainable feeling of happiness and healing that we all feel as we approach the barn and our horses friendly nicker.

However Lunas story isn't the same as everyone else. She came from a mistreated youth, leaving her scarred emotionally and weary of everyone. She was labeled as dangerous; and seemingly tried to live up to her name as such.   Veterinarians wouldn't treat her, farriers wouldn't shoe her, no one would get near her without sedation, chains and/or whips. In the simple task of turning in and out, it took two people on either side of her with chains and whips.   However, this is not a story of her daunting past, it is a story of what and where love, dedication, passion and patience can turn a mean, crazy and dangerous horse into as of yesterday will be schooling as a third level dressage horse.

I still remember the first time I rode Luna, I had just returned from Marshall and Sterling national finals and had had my last hurrah with my 15.2 appendix Beau. It was time to work on a horse more size appropriate for me at 5'7 and I wanted a challenge.

The difficult horses teach you the most, do they not? Luna had just arrived at Providence Equestrian Center, a beautiful 16.2 gray Oldenburg. Mind you to this point in time I had never been a fan of

grays, but she had a presence about her. Granted this presence was not necessarily that of roses and rainbows, but there was something
about her that I was drawn to. My trainer Bob Braren had known Luna
through her colorful past and was less than thrilled that she was taken on at Providence mainly for his fear for the safety of anyone around her. I didn't care though, I wanted to ride her and I was up for the challenge of changing her into what some may refer to as a "normal" horse. Goodness knows   I wasn't fully

aware of the task at hand, I just knew I was up for it!

For the first six months of riding her, it was a challenge to just get her feet unglued and moving forward. She would kick, stomp, crow hop and buck just to let you know that she wasn't happy with you telling her what to do. Crazy enough, I believe it was just a few weeks into those shenanigans that I had decided I wanted her to be mine.

At the time I was going through a deployment with a loved one and needed anything that would take my mind and concentration off of the severity at hand. Perfect! A horse that was trying to kill me would definitely need all of my time and attention.

The months dragged on like molasses. Although we finally were able to begin our warm up without a battle, that was only if nothing had been moved, touched, or altered in any way shape or fashion; up to and including the time of day, day of the week, temperature, moon phases, etc. Needless to say "my" horse was neurotic, high strung, scared, opinionated, stubborn and extremely sensitive. To everything. We had at that point figured out that there was no telling this horse. She was a princess and demanded that she be asked to do anything and not only asked, you had to fool her to think that it was her idea all along. Talk about being having to become the thinking rider. Not only was my body being challenged in skill and having to stay seated throughout the bucks and mishaps, my mind had to be fully engaged predicting her every movement while I may or may not of been trying to ask her to do something different. I had never been challenged like that and had it not been for Bob I never would of learned how to do

so. Its through his communication with the horse and ability to translate it to me that had made the journey that far worth it.

Things then started to fall in to place. I worked with Luna six days a week and was finally able to properly communicate with her, for the most part at least. She still tried to launch me at least once a day, but had not been successful.

That was short lived as on Christmas Eve Luna decided to give me my Christmas present early and sent me, as Bob referred to it as 15,000 feet and flying. I came crashing down on my wrists and luckily I escaped with only a sprain. Just a pretty nasty one. To date though, that has been the only injury (knock on wood!) she has inflicted upon me.

In no time things were able to proceed as normal. I was still getting bucked and nearly spooked out of my seat on a consistent basis, Bob still thought I was crazy, I still wanted to buy her, and she seemingly wanted nothing to do with anything. I still loved her, I couldn't get enough of her sass, and after learning of her story of neglect and mistreatment I could only see her as a reflection of myself through my youth.

That summer of 2012 turmoil had struck my life. It wasn't until that point in time where I had really seen and felt the depth of the relationship that I had with this horse. Sparing the details, my fiance had returned from war only to break up with me, shattering my heart and any plans that I had had for my future. The only thing I had at the point in time was Luna. I would sit in her stall and cry for hours on end and without hesitation she took over the role of my protector and alpha in my time of weakness.

This dangerous horse would stand over me, hooves within inches of my weakened body, nuzzling my head and breathing not only into my ear, but my heart and soul as well. She would pin her ears and snarl at anyone who came close to me and would block me from anything that she perceived as a threat. If I hadn't wanted her before this was the nail in the coffin. I did not care who tried to tell me

different or sway my judgment, this was going to be my horse. I would figure out a way eventually.

It was time to rebuild myself, get out of my own head and give back to this horse what she had provided me. Love, empathy and respect. We worked our tails off, six days a week. Every day was a little bit better than the past, but it was on a very slow incline. Kind of like the bunny hill on a ski mountain. That's ok though, I had nothing but time and energy to throw into her. Finally August came around and we decided it was time to make our show debut. Something as a starting point and excel from since up to that point in time it had either been through my rose colored glasses or Bobs realistic expectations. If you can imagine we often sat on opposites sides of the fence. Everyone was on board at this point in time and we were off to not only our first show, but a rated one at Fox Lea taboot.

Fox Lea offers USDF opportunity classes in training level test one and two, which is an affordable (and highly suggested!) option to be judged at rated level. The only difference is that you would not be able to use your scores towards any USDF title or points. No big deal, we were going for the experience and the watchful eye of a "tougher" judge. With bad weather upon us, we only showed one day of the weekend, but were able to pick up a second and fourth place with scores of (if I'm not mistaken) a 63+ and 59+ respectively. Nothing to write home about, but also nothing to snub your nose at. This was our very first dressage show and even with all her neurosis she still was the best that she was capable of being at that point in time.

Back to the farm and back to the grind. We knew we had our work cut out for us, but there was nothing but time to improve upon it. That is until a fated day in early October took her out for the next four and a half months. She was being used as a school horse in one of the hunter lessons and unbeknownst to the girl riding, we was using a saddle with a broken tree. For over forty minutes my poor Luna had been repeatably stabbed in her withers with the highly infectious pine that saddles are made of. At first it didn't look too bad, maybe an over

sized spider bite, but that quickly changed in the days to follow. I had been treating the wound and on day 3 I noticed things had taken a

turn for the worse. She had swelled up over the area so much that she looked like a camel and she was showing signs of colic believed to be from the pain she was experiencing. The vet was called and she was prescribed an antibiotic immediately.

Another couple days passed and as I arrived to the barn one morning I saw what may of been the most disturbing and disgusting things on a horse possible, The swelling was now protruding about an inch from her body and was now in the shape of a saddle, with one side of her completely covered in a thick, yellow, oozing puss. I literally started gagging and immediately called the head trainer at the farm. Antibiotics were not cutting it at the point in time and the doctor was called to come down for a farm visit that afternoon. He dug out the wound and left us with strict directions on how to keep it clean and away from any further infection.

It was still unknown if she had broken her withers, but the most important thing was to stop the spread of the infection causing her to become septic. As the days went on I spent as much time as possible with her, the day we feared colic I stayed with her overnight in her stall. It was one thing after another and seemingly never going to end as proud flesh kept returning and it was nearly impossible to keep the bandage on. Four months of eternity passed, the wound was finally sealing closed and the infection was gone.

While I wish we had never lost those four plus months, I am grateful for the time to prove to her that I will always be there to take care of her. No one else sat with her for hours, she was merely treated and left alone in the back of the barn in her stall, Most of the treatment was administered by me as well. Our bond was only strengthened through the ordeal and the day I put that saddle pad and surcingle on her back was one of my happiest that year. Finally within a couple weeks later we were back under saddle and slowly back to work! Albeit a bit nervous, I felt like I was flying when we were finally able to canter again. Unfortunately that too was short lived as two months

later I received a phone call while on my way to farm that began with
"don't worry but..." Don't worry but, that instantaneously gives me reason to worry. Luna had somehow sliced open the side of her left hind, hock to nearly her fetlock. She did about ten percent damage to her suspensory ligament and had a small un-repairable part removed. Great, not only another injury, but a dressage horse with a damaged suspensory ligament? I wasn't going to leave her side though, she was after all "my" horse. After two weeks I was finally able to hand walk her for short dur-ation's of time. This wound took far less time to heal and after roughly eight weeks I was removing her last stitch and back under saddle.

Back to work again. At this point in time it was clear to me without a reason or doubt that I was to buy this horse. I could not imagine my life without my Lunabear and one faith-ful night in September 2013 I was emailed and prompted with the opportunity to do as such. By now I had already gone over all my bank accounts, finances and bills, figuring that it may be tight but that I would be able to afford her. Bob admittedly still against the purchase with his thoughts that she may not pro-gress past a certain level agreed to join me in a meeting with Heather regarding my offering price. It was nerve wrecking, but I knew I had the advantage. No one could ride this horse the way I could and I loved her with all my heart which was evi-dent through my care and admiration. I proclaimed I would own Luna for the rest of her life and that was the determining statement which sealed our fate and accepting what some may consider a measly sum of money. That day was September 10th, I will always and forever remember that day. I, Kristin Peterson, the girl with only dreams of owning a horse for 26 years had finally made it come true.

With the gigantic new expense of owning a horse now on my shoulders, I went out to seek further employment. Without fail, my incredible trainer Bob Braren came through for me again, introducing me to Julie Griffin and the beautiful Whimsical Farms. It was only a couple weeks of having to commute from my house in Fort Myers, to

my horse in Bonita Springs, to my job in Alva at the farm, to my "real" job managing Cirellas Italian Bistro and Sushi bar back in Bonita, that
I realized it was time to relocate my horse out to the farm I was working at so I could see her as much as possible. Even if I couldn't ride I would still be able to be around her. I missed her when I was around all the new horses at Whimsical and she was by her lonesome in Bonita.

Once we arrived to our new home at Whimsical Farms the forward progress was almost immediate and instantaneous. This by far was the best move I am sure that has ever occurred in this horses life. Through the introduction to our new farm friends, grass, turnout and a large stall, we were also introduced to an all natural, holistic approach to everything from everyday maintenance to treating viruses and grief. Dr. Gerald Wessner has successfully peeled back the layers of onion being my Luna and treated her for the fraction of the cost of your average large animal veterinarian and in an all natural and healthier way. If I hadn't experienced with my own two eyes I would too still be a skeptic. Whenever Luna seems to be exhibiting off behaviors or discomfort, all it takes is for her to know that I called Dr. Wessner to display happier expressions and sense of ease.

The change in Luna and the horse she has become today is absolutely incredible. With a few of our local SWFDA shows, including winning our first blue ribbon at one of said shows (!!), under our belt we made our way back to Fox Lea Farms for another shot at a rated show. It still brings tears to my eyes when I think about the joy I experienced that weekend. For lack of better words we absolutely killed it both days. Our lowest score was on Saturday in training level test two was a 65+% and a second place, and our highest score was on Sunday again in training level test two, but this time with a 73+% and a second blue for the weekend! We also were entered into an open professional class for training level test three and up to some pretty tough competition we held our own bringing in a fourth place (of seven) and a 66+%! Unbeknownst to the judges their comments on

my scorecard were probably some of the most touching words anyone has ever written about us. "Elegant horse," "capable pair,"
"hardworking horse," were just a few. We received 8's on all of our tests for gaits and a few for harmony between horse and rider. It was just magical.

Its so beautiful and practically, if you can imagine, unexplainable to portray the relationship that I have with my Luna. Alongside Bob, this horse has taught me almost everything I know, and through her vices given me the knowledge to solve nearly any issue any horse can give me. Chances are shes given it to me more often and at times worse. Would I change it though? Never. We have proven the fact that through hard work anything is truly possible. Just the other day we began work towards schooling at third level. Third level! A horse that for the first six months of working with her wouldn't even walk forward is now capable to do a pirouette type canter for the entire length of a ring in a three loop serpentine. Point of the story, don't give up on that dream. Don't give up on that horse. Dreams don't work unless you do, and who knows, that horse may of just chosen you, you can't explain it, but they know exactly what they are doing.

THE CHANGELING

Submitted By JANICE

As a young girl, I had always wanted a leopard appaloosa. But didn't have any luck finding one I could afford. I had saved and scrimped to try to afford the horse of my dreams.

My grandfather, an old horseman from way back, knew I had tried everything I could to find my dream horse, and told me to never give up, that I would have that app one day!

Well, year after year, my dream slipped further and further away. I had given up all hope by the time I was 16. I looked at my measly pile of money and decided to just get another horse. Let me interject here that my family already had a few horses, but none were just mine, they were for the farm. Work horses and plow horses.

One day, my grandfather called me downstairs and said that someone had left something for me in the barn! I ran out there with not a clue of what to expect! But my grand fathers smile was shining!

I walked into the barn, and there in a stall stood the ugliest colt I had ever seen! He was all black with whitish rings around his eyes, and on his muzzle! I wasn't sure what was going on with this colt, but my grandfather came in behind me, still grinning ear to ear. I asked him what this colt was, and in his knowing and old timers way, he just smiled and said "He's yours". It turns out that a man who knew my grandfather, had heard this colt was going through the slaughter auction, although in that day they weren't as well known as they are today. He called my grandfather and asked him to take this guy because it was a shame to see him go like that! And my grandfather naturally said yes.

Well, he wasn't the Leopard app that I had dreamed of, but he was mine! I started his training right away! Teaching him to stand in crossties and be groomed, and have his feet done! He was so sweet and gentle that in no time he was following me everywhere around the farm. But something strange started to happen.... He started losing his black coat! He was turning white! The ugly white rings around his eyes

disappeared, and within the first few months, he turned into the LEOPARD APPALOOSA I had dreamed of!

My grandfather already knew he would, having raised apps for years, and he knew what this colt would be! I was the happiest girl in the world and soon starter showing him in fun shows! AND WINNING! Halter class! As soon as he was old enough to break, he took it like a champ!

We had 28 years together, and have never had another horse. I didn't need to, because the one I had was perfect!

SWAMP DONKEY

Submitted by JASON

A few years ago, my buddies and I were air boating in the everglades, near Miami. We had been out most of the day, when a call came over the radio from another friend who said there was a donkey stuck in the middle of the glades.

We jetted over there thinking he had maybe had one too many! But when we got there, he wasn't kidding, there was a little donkey standing chest deep stuck in the mud!

How he got there we will never know, as it was in the MIDDLE of no where, with no service roads or anything near by! And, yes, gators were very near. My buddy had been keeping them away as best he could until we got there.

We all tried to figure out how to get this little guy out of the mud and out of the swamp. We finally decided to use the paddle we had to try to give him some leverage to get unstuck and then try to get him on one of the boats.

Well, getting him unstuck was the easy part. Trying to get him onto a boat, not so much. He refused to budge...stubborn little creatures. But soon he was exhausted trying to fight, and let us pick him up and put him on the boat. We were worried he would freak out when the motor started, but he was so tired, he lay in the floor of the boat and never moved until we got back to base camp.

We unloaded him, and my friend Bill had a truck with a cap. Soooo, into the truck bed he went and locked safely in by the cap door, we loaded out gear and discussed what to do with him. Bill has a few acres so he said he would take him until we could find his owners.

We called everyone we could think of and placed ads trying to find out who owned him. No owner ever came forward. So Bill now has a new buddy who actually is a sweet little guy and loves Bill's grandchildren! Giving them rides around the farm, and eating Bill's wife's flowers!

He is never going anywhere. Bill loves his little swamp donkey!

ABANDONED

Submitted By JESSICA H.

M iami has it's share of lost or abandoned animals. That includes livestock. Working in the deep recesses of Miami- I have seen several goats, sheep, ponies, cows and horses left dead on the side of the roads, or in canals where people had left them to either die or had already died.

Sadly, a lot of these animals have been used as sacrifices for religious ceremonies, and the bodies discarded afterwards. We have found parts of animals, heads, pelts etc... just thrown into the canals.

Also, we have found live animals discarded in the deep recesses of the swamps and farm land as well. This story is about one of those horses.

We got a call from someone who had been hiking back in the glades on one of the service roads. He said there was a pile of dead animals out there that looked recent. So my team got on it and headed out. When we arrived ,we saw a pile of goats, donkeys, chickens, dogs, and some we could not identify. We were standing there taking pictures of everything for documentation when we saw a slight movement in the middle of the pile. One of the guys on the team started moving bodies to see what could be alive underneath of the pile. When we got to the middle, we found a foal!

This little thing, so emaciated, hollow eyed, and couldn't stand, broke our hearts! We lifted her into our arms, luckily she was a mini, and rushed her back to one of the trucks. The rest of the team stayed behind to finish documenting the pile of animals.

We rushed her to our vet who began emergency treatment on her. He thought she was actually going to be ok if she made it through the next 48 hours!

There was nothing more we could do, so we headed back out to the pile, and began clean up. It was absolutely heartbreaking! All of these animals had been either starved, or used in rituals. Heads missing, and parts gone. But sadly, we come across this more than we should in this area. It is so remote, and there are no houses or cameras in the area! So for people to just dump their animals is a pretty regular thing.

After we had clean up done and reports filed, I went to the vet's office to check on the foal. She seemed to be doing well! Everyone there had already fallen in love with her, and were all pulling for her! By the 48 hour deadline, she was bright eyed and doing amazing! She was going to pull through!

We ran the story on the news asking for tips to try to find who had dumped these animals, and we were going to try to find the owner and press charges!

About a week later we got an anonymous tip about a man who had a farm not too far from where we found the animals, who sold animals for sacrifice rituals. He did not speak any English, so fortunately, one of our team spoke his language.

When we rolled up to his place, the smell alone was enough to make your eyes water! There were all kinds of animals standing around in mud and muck, skinny, no fresh water, and no food! We saw dead animals laying all over the place. When we started talking to the man, he said that he just sells them to other Cubans for meat and sacrifice. He said he wasn't going to put any money into something that was just going to be killed anyway. When we asked him about the animals he had dumped in the pile, he said the baby was in the way, and he wanted to breed the mare back to get a colt. He didn't want a filly! That is why he took her and dumped her along with the dead animals.

After a lot of haggling, he finally showed us the mare, and we were shocked. She was in horrible shape, maggots eating her flesh, open sores all over her body, tail so matted with manure it was a solid brick. Hooves so overgrown she couldn't walk. And she was stuck in a large dog cage. Not a chain link kennel, but a dog cage, like you would put a dog in inside the house! He finally agreed to give her to us, and we quickly loaded her into our truck and rushed her to our vet. On the way our other team, the ones who handle abuse cases was on the way to his place.

As soon as we unloaded her at the office, we helped her into the exam room, where the whole staff prepared her for treatment. Her foal

was still there as well, and when brought out to see her mom, her little eyes lit up and it was all the tech could do to get her to walk, not run to her. At the same time, her mom, whose head hung nearly to the ground with defeat, brightened up, and let out quite the whinny to see her baby!

The two stayed for about another week at the veterinarian, and were released with a long road ahead of them, but one of the girls on our team adopted them both and a year later they are doing great!

It saddens me to see how many horses end up dumped in

the swamps, but occasionally we find them and are able to help!

DROPPED IN HIS TRACKS

Submitted by ISHKARI

I am from a village in Turkey. I see a lot of my people using horses for work here, and it is our custom to do so. We are a poor area and can not afford tractors and truck and other farming tools. Everything we do is by hand. We do not have the luxury of machines to make hay for us, or pull our crops. So we use horses. And I have to say that most of our horses are well cared for. But there are always a few that aren't cared for. This is about one of those.

I was walking in our village when I saw a man beating a horse pulling a cart up a very steep hill. The horse was having a hard time getting the heavy load up the hill, and was giving it everything he had. But the road was muddy and rocky, and the horse just didn't have what it took to get the heavy load up there.

A group of us stopped to watch, and felt horrible for the horse who was trying as hard as he could! The man kept beating on him trying to make him do something he just could not do.

Finally, a large man stepped forward, and took the whip from the cruel owner. The owner and he talked for a minute, and the man unhitched to horse from the cart and a couple of other men started unloading the cart, and helped the man get his cart up the hill. The horse just lay exhausted in the mud. When the got his cart up the hill, and had reloaded it with the things they had taken off, the men then helped him get his cart home. The horse forgotten about in the mud.

The large man who stopped the beating, and I got the horse unstuck, and to his feet. The man said that he was taking the horse home, and he would never endure suck cruelty again.

A few months later, I saw the large man in town. His 4 children perched atop the horse the man had saved! We talked for a while and he said his children love the horse, and the horse loves them! The horse has a great forever home, and kids who love him!

STANLEY

Submitted By CASSANDRA

Trash. That is what Stanley was to the kill pen owner. A half starved, lame old horse. What can I say, I had to have him. The owner of the pen took the $100 I offered for him and I brought him home. The man had told me he probably would not live another 48 hours. But I could not leave him there, covered in mud, open wounds and skin sloughing off his poor emaciated old body.

Well, he made it. And after the vet came out and looked him over, it turned out Stanley was only 10~! We had a long road ahead of us to get him back in shape, but we were in it for life! So we began an uphill journey with him! It took a good year to get him back to a happy horse! But it was so worth it!

I found out that he had been a reigning horse! He still had all the moves! We found out completely by accident! He was out in the pasture playing around, doing sliding stops, and spins! I have a friend who shows reiners and he came by to have a look! He watched Stanley playing alone out there and we brought him in and tacked him up so my friend could try him out! After a while of warm ups, the real exhibition began! He truly was a reigning horse!

My friend started teaching us together, and by the next season, we decided to try our hand at showing! Surprising everyone, we were winning in novice!

My little $100 horse was a champion in the ring! He loved

doing it, and so did I! It was amazing to watch our videos and see the joy in his eyes as he was sliding to a stop!

Several years later, he is truly an old man, and is living out his life in my pasture at 28 years old!

◆ ◆ ◆

I would like to thank everyone who contributed their stories for this book. I am so glad that the horses in these stories were able to be saved and have a good life until the end.

I would like to write another book in the future, so if your story did not make it into this one, perhaps it will make it into the next!

Also, if you could not contribute a story at this time, you can still email your stories to horserescuestories@gmail.com and I will get back to you regarding the next book!

As I said, some of the proceeds from this book will be going to horse rescues so they can continue their amazing work for the horses we love so much!

Again, thank you!

Carrie

Printed in Great Britain
by Amazon

53508050R00108